THE
PATH
TO
LIGHT

PHEELLO NTUKA

THE
PATH
TO
LIGHT

INSPIRED
PUBLISHING

The Path To Light

First Edition, First Impression 2019

ISBN 978-0-6398256-4-9

Copyright © Pheello Ntuka

Published by: Inspired Publishing

PO Box 82058 | Southdale | 2135 Johannesburg , South Africa

Email: info@inspiredpublishing.co.za

www.inspiredpublishing.co.za

DEDICATION

This book is dedicated to everyone who seeks success, joy and inner peace and the ordinary men and women who are affected by the system of "unconscious incompetence" which simply means "not knowing that you do not know."

When knowledge is practiced, it turns into experience which then becomes wisdom.

I am forever grateful for having learnt and experienced these 10 transformational principles, this is my wish for you too.

TABLE OF CONTENTS

Acknowledgments 1

Introduction.. 3

PART 1: SEARCH FOR YOUR INNER-SELF...................... 9

Chapter 1: Life Purpose Is Key To Your Final Destination.. 11

Chapter 2: Learn How To Detach And Let Go 31

Chapter 3: How Grateful Are You? 43

PART 2: CONTINUOUS LEARNING 57

Chapter 4: Food For The Mind 59

Chapter 5: Today's Habits Affect Your Tomorrow 75

Chapter 6: The Power Of Choices 87

PART 3:UNDERSTAND YOUR INNER POWER 105

Chapter 7: Emotions Are A Powerful Driving Force.......... 107

Chapter 8: Review Your Belief System 123

Chapter 9: Improve Self-Discipline 141

Chapter 10: Miracles Of Massive Action........................... 155

Acknowledgments

I wish to extend a special word of gratitude to everyone who con- tributed towards the success of this massive project. Writing this book started as a dream, and today I am so delighted to confirm that dreams do come true.

To the Almighty God, thank You for all the blessings, the life and the strength you have provided me since the beginning of my life.

Special thanks to my beautiful wife Malerato for the everlasting love, support and prayers.

To my daughters Amohelang, Atlehang, Kutloano and Sentle, you will always be my pillar of strength and I love you with all my heart. To my mentors and coaches Bishop Abe Sibiya, Pastor Abishai Mo- agi, Mr. Themba Maseko and Mr. Brendon Govender, thank you for the words of encouragement and inspiration, I am forever grateful for your support.

To Mr. Darren August and Inspired Publishing, thank you for making my long-awaited dream a reality.

Thank you, Thank You and Thank You.

Introduction

Born and raised in a small township, with no major developments and growth, called Sharpeville near Vereeniging. I have always wondered why some people become more successful and happier than others when we all live in the same city, same township and probably attended the same schools. This question kept rolling at the back of my mind for many years. As years passed by, my curiosity grew stronger. Even in the workplace today, you still find people becoming more successful and happier than others. I started studying the life patterns of the minority who always seem happier, more successful and mostly at peace than the majority.

Have you ever felt like you are working very hard and doing everything right but getting frustrated due to minimum results that steal your joy and inner peace? To me, frustration means expecting extraordinary result without becoming extraordinary. I have seen this a lot in my work environment. Most people rely on hope, they wish and pray that they get a high salary and get promoted but they are not willing to become more valuable by increasing their skills and knowledge. One critical principle that I really believe in is, what is more important is the value you bring, and the value you accrue - more than what you are getting; for it is who you become that attracts greater rewards and therefore brings you joy and inner peace.

One of the major challenges we have as a society is being afraid to change our present way of doing things, even when we do not get the results we are expecting from our efforts. We settle for the unwanted outcomes from our hard work, which leads us into confusion and frustration, this surely steals our joy and inner peace.

The 10 transformational principles in this book have changed my life drastically and transitioned me from darkness to light, moved me from minimum results to massive results and continue to perform miracles in my life. I believe they will continue to do so in years to come. I strongly believe these basic and profound principles will do the same to everyone who will make time to learn and apply them in their lives. A principle is simply a rule that controls how something works and is supposed to function. Our lives are also designed to follow certain laws and rules so we can function effectively and get maximum results. These basic principles will guarantee you success, joy and inner peace. Just by changing your current way of doing things which perhaps is not producing positive results. This book provides light on how to redesign your own life philosophy so that it ensures success, joy and inner peace.

The importance of having inner peace is immeasurable. When you attain it, you know that you have made it. You now fully understand the meaning of life, view the world very differently and you start seeing life for what it is all about – life is about two important words, growth and contribution. Here is a quote by William Shakespeare: "The meaning of life is to find your gift, the purpose of life is to give it away". You start being grateful for the little things life has already offered you. You develop an appreciation for the things you have taken for granted in the past such as the air we breathe, the rain, the soil, the sun and the seeds, the trees and beautiful gardens.

The world on its own is a wonderful place to be. I have learnt that simplicity is always key. Life was made to be simple and yet profound, until we made it complex.

Having peace of mind means being at ease and enjoying the power of calmness. When everyone is rushing and feeling overwhelmed, you take it slow and have more control. When you have inner-peace, you become clear on what is more important.

Anthony Robbins says, "Success without fulfilment is ultimate failure." My own understanding of success is knowing where you are going and slowly progressing towards that direction. The accumulation of the little activities that lead to your major goal.

I cannot over emphasize the importance of finding joy and inner peace. It is incomparable to anything in this world. Applying the 10 basic principles in this book will help you find that peace you have been looking for.

This book is for anyone who wants success, joy and peace within, everyone who wants to enjoy and experience life with minimum and controllable fear, life full of love and happiness.

My desire is that the lessons in the following chapters help you transform and add value to your current life and improve the way you see the world. I strongly believe in the basics, the principles and the laws of life, and would like to be remembered as Mr. Basic principles. You have probably heard and seen these life principles before and may be familiar with them, which is ok. There is power deep inside these basic principles.

All I ask is that you read all the chapters in this book with the intention of pondering these critical basic principles and slowly refining your current life philosophy. Do apply what you think might be appropriate and worth implementing in your life and get to your own new well- designed destination full of peace, success, joy and happiness. My guarantee is that these principles as basic as they are, will redirect anyone to the path to light.

As you read on you will notice that all the 10 transformational principles in this book are related, just like the body and soul. One principle cannot function well without the others.

"Where there is knowledge, there is light, and where there is light, there is abundance of wisdom, therefore empower your life philosophy and take the path to light." -Pheello Ntuka

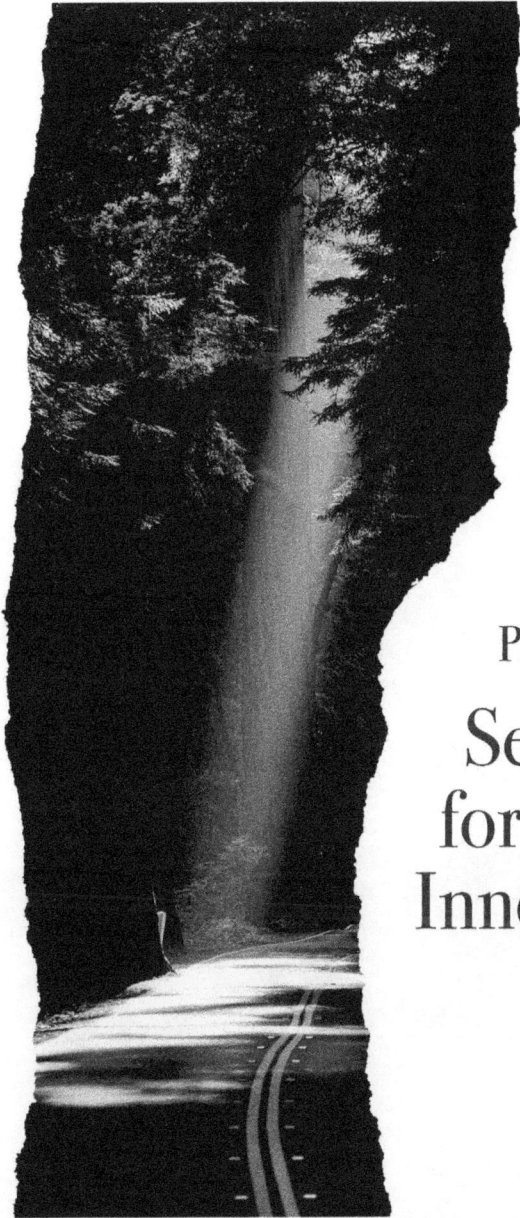

PART 1

Search
for your
Inner-Self

CHAPTER 1

Life Purpose is Key to your Final Destination

_____

According to the Cambridge dictionary, purpose is defined as why something exists. My own meaning of purpose is the uniqueness or function of something to serve something else. Others simply call it a "calling", or "life calling." Purpose is the original intent of a product to perform its manufacturer's original function. It is what the product was designed for and what it must do or perform. Our aim in life is to uncover the reasons why we are in this world, planet earth. It is your "why" for living.

Through personal development, I have learnt a lot in more than five years of research and studying the life patterns of happy, peaceful and successful people. I am still amazed by the feeling of completeness, calmness and love that I am experiencing in my life as a result of the principles that I write about in this book. In this chapter I will share the very first basic principle of finding inner peace, which is the core foundation for finding your inner-self. My simple meaning of inner-self is our "internal world" which includes but is not limited to self-talk, self-image and how we communicate with the outside world. The subject of inner-self is a wide one and is very helpful when learning more about who we really are. I spent over sixteen years of my adult life working hard with no visible positive results, just survival. Travelling back and forth for about 110 kilometers daily from south of Johannesburg to Centurion. On most days, I found myself stuck in traffic, getting frustrated and not knowing what to do to change my situation. This frustration, which grew year after year, kept stealing my joy and inner peace - for I didn't really know what to do to change and correct my situation. Life was getting tougher and stressful for me; my shift work grew more demanding and tiring. Motorists on the N1 could be unpredictable, judgmental and coldhearted. I felt confused and overwhelmed most of the time. I was not coping with all these challenges very well.

Moving closer to Centurion was not an option as it was going to massively affect my family and our general lifestyle. Making major changes is not always easy when you have a big family like mine. My wife would have to look for another job in Centurion or closer, the children would need to change schools. This was going to be a major change we were all not prepared to go through. I knew deeply in my heart that I had to do something. The situation was constantly affecting me mentally and emotionally. Every day felt like I was moving far away from my loved ones as they are all depending on me. Part of me always knew and kept reminding me that Johannesburg was not where I grew up until I became a young adult, Sharpeville.

LIVING LIFE WITHOUT PURPOSE

The feeling of emptiness that was growing inside me due to my limited knowledge of what I was born to do, and my lack of future plans was enough for me to start searching for better options.

Our lives can be changed by life's challenges. The subject of, "The day that changed my life", is a very wide one. Change happens to every living organism including human beings. Challenges such as finding yourself in a constant state of embarrassment, disgust, losing respect, low self-esteem, low self-confidence and losing trust in someone you love are enough to make a change in your life. When you constantly break promises to family and loved ones, this can lead you to a point where you say these familiar words, "Enough is enough."

This is exactly what happened to me. I was working very hard, stuck in traffic daily, feeling overwhelmed and confused, constantly breaking my promises, sometimes observing horrible accidents and knowing that it could be me one day. The worst part is that I was not really seeing any improvement in my life, I was consistently in the rat-race. I could not wait to be off shift hoping that I would enjoy my weekend off. I only realized and learnt that the reason I was getting frustrated and confused by all this was because I didn't have a specific purpose and vision in my life. I had not found my reason for living, and by default I was doing as the Jones do. I had not yet found what I was born to do, and this severely affected my destiny.

This realization motivated me to start looking for better ways of effectively dealing with all the challenges in my life. I knew that it was time for me to start analyzing and refining my life philosophy by applying some wise changes that would improve not only my life, but that of my family as well. Nothing is worse than a financially broke father with low self-esteem or a husband with no future plans. In recent years I learnt that every family needs a man with great future plans. I believe the best question to ask a man before entering in any kind of relationship or marriage is, "What are your current and future plans?" The second question is, "Where exactly are you leading us to?" These questions simply mean what is your purpose and vision in life?

I started with what I call "Personal Development and Self Education", this is what I strongly believe changed my life. It gave me more joy, inner peace and stability. Most of us usually think that we know it all after graduating from college or university, until we start experiencing the reality of life. This is where there is no teacher or lecturer to guide you. You now have to make critical decisions about life, daily duties, finances and health, family, the future - the list is endless.

You now realize that your knowledge is still very limited, and that education alone is not enough to live a happy and peaceful life. I started doing research on topics such as happiness, inner peace, mental strength, emotions, love, family, finance, health, successful living, self-motivation, career, management and business. I started attending short courses on life transformation and coaching, learning more on life philosophy and general personal development. I started collecting specific books and built my "home library." I am still amazed by the information one can get by reading books from those people who are already happy, successful and living peaceful lives.

ANALYZE AND REFINE YOUR LIFE PURPOSE

The moment you find your life purpose, you suddenly begin to slowdown in this super-fast-paced and busy life we find ourselves in. By slowing down, your mind has less to worry about. Your life choices become clearer and focused, the decisions you make bring you joy and inner peace. The key thought is "Clarity is Power." When you are at peace with yourself, you think and feel better, love and accept yourself unconditionally and you enjoy your life. We were all born with nothing in our hands and we will also go to the grave with nothing. The only thing we can offer others while we are still alive is our unique skills, talents, knowledge and life lessons which we have learnt as we were growing up and experiencing different challenges of life. Serving others and using our skills and talents to help those who need assistance to improve their lives is one of many ways of serving our life purpose. One day you too will die with nothing in your hands anyway, all your acquired material wealth and possessions won't follow you to your last place of rest. Why not share your unique life lessons or simply help others who really need assistance?

As human beings in this world, we are all different yet equally important. Each and every one of us has a special skill or talent to offer, I believe God created us differently on purpose. Life wouldn't be joyful and challenging if we were all identical in thought, action and behavior. The importance of finding your sole purpose is critical in reducing the overwhelming effect of the activities we find ourselves having to do on a daily basis.

By helping you focus on specific important issues in your life which in return reduce the pressure of trying to do everything all by yourself with no results. This reduces unnecessary tension and pressure from the people you are involved with in your environment. The minute you find your sole purpose, you start working on important goals that you have identified as critical. You break down your goals into small pieces and phases, set your priorities well, making it enjoyable and simpler to achieve. It is therefore very significant to regularly analyze and refine your life purpose.

SOME EXAMPLES OF LIFE PURPOSE AND HOW THEY ARE IDENTIFIED

Your own life purpose is first identified as something you really have great passion for. Passion is the sum of your major interest plus repetition, meaning the more you do what you are interested in, the more passion you create. If you follow your strong interest and your burning desire towards something, this will soon develop and become your passion. Sometimes you might have to add passion to the very same thing you are busy with, like your current job for instance. Sometimes just by putting a little bit of passion to your business, talent, job or skills, this could be enough to turn things around. In South Africa we have people who have passion in different fields. We have teachers, church ministers, Priest, Pastors and Bishops, authors, actors, public speakers, managers, cleaners, supervisors, landscapers, nurses, government officials, politicians, leaders in different businesses, plumbers, electricians, motivational speakers, sports athletes, comedians, musicians, producers, the list is endless.

Whatever your passion is or whatever skill you can use to effectively serve people with joy. If you have something you can do whole heartedly without even thinking of getting paid for it or without expecting any reward, this may very well be a hint of where your purpose may lie. It may start as a hobby but with time, practice and wisdom; you may eventually be able to make it financially rewarding, especially if it is something that adds value to the lives of others.

When we look at all the great leaders from the bible, all of them were serving people in different ways even before they stepped into fulfilling God's special purpose of leading the people of the Lord to a specific path and destination. These leaders were created to achieve a mission from God. From this, I conclude that God also wants us to serve his purpose by leading his people to greatness. We can accomplish this through serving and providing value to his people by simply helping one another. Every manufacturer designs and creates products for a specific purpose, similarly, I believe, our Creator had the same idea of specific purpose when He created us. A simple principle that I apply in my life is that success comes from helping as many people as possible.

———————————

The following questions helped me discover my life purpose and I believe they can help you too. Take some time and try to answer the following questions, keeping your answers as brief and simple as you can.

Who are you?

This question is very important for it defines who you really are in your own internal world and is key when you are still searching for your purpose.

I have learnt that I am not my name and I am also not the body, my names were given to me by my parents and they are just words, the body on the other side is the "vehicle" carrying the wonderful assets in my internal world and therefore need to be taken care of.

My belief is that I am a spiritual creature, having the mind and emotions, living in a physical body that was created by the Almighty Creator who is my source of life and I am his resource in this world. This is who I am.

Knowing who you are helps you deal better with the outside world and gives you more control over your daily life challenges.

_____

_____

_____

_____

_____

_____

_____

_____

What do you do?

What are you known for?

This defines your own mission and purpose.

_____

_____

_____

_____

_____

_____

_____

_____

_____

_____

_____

_____

_____

Who do you do it for?

Do you do what you do for the children, community, adults, orphans etc.? This defines the people you are serving.

_____

_____

_____

_____

_____

_____

_____

Why do you do what you do?

List all possible reasons for doing what you do, the more reasons you have, the stronger your sense of purpose and the more you will persevere when you experience difficulty and feel like you want to give up. These reasons will pull you through, and you will stand up and go on.

_____

_____

_____

_____

_____

_____

_____

_____

What do they want or need?

What do these people you are serving need and what solutions are you providing to them?

_____

_____

_____

_____

_____

_____

_____

_____

How do they change as a result?

Is your purpose adding any value?

Now and then review your progress and keep improving.

There is a great feeling accompanied by simply helping others, no matter how small. This is my interpretation and understanding of serving your life purpose.

_____

_____

_____

_____

_____

_____

_____

SIMPLICITY IS KEY

Through personal development and self-education, I have learnt more about myself, my passions, belief system, values, real interests and my inner-self. Knowing my purpose has incredibly improved my life and given it meaning. Knowing and having your sole purpose is like having a filter, separating all the unwanted information and negative emotions trying to enter into your life or your mind. This results in fewer worries and challenges to focus on, allowing life to become simpler. The newfound inner-peace and relaxed mind helps in generating good ideas.

I have experienced confusion and uncertainty in life, and this usually complicates everything. Things that are supposed to be very simple, like having fun with your family, your relationships and economic related issues are affected. The world we live in is unpredictable. It is therefore important to eliminate all unnecessary issues that could affect everything you do. Having a clear life purpose will highlight for you what is trivial and allow you to focus on what is more significant to you. Most people find themselves going in all directions trying or looking for all opportunities, even those that are not related to where they want to go.

The key lesson here is learning how to keep your life simple and do only what is significant. Simplicity ultimately provides joy and peace within, the life with no complications with less stress and confusion, increasing the success rate of achieving your goals.

PURPOSE AND VISION

The day I understood the power of having a purpose that is linked to a vision, my life radically changed for the better. Purpose says, "This is what I am here for and this is what I do", while vision says,

"Here is the path I am taking to the address of my final destination." When I explain this principle to teenagers and young adults, I put it this way: "Purpose is simply what the manufacturer created the product to do and vision is simply the laws set by the manufacturer to be followed and adhered to, so the intended outcome of the product can be achieved."

I believe there is a reason why our Creator made our fingerprints different, for our purpose in life is also very unique. There is power in our individuality, we might be doing the same function or similar jobs, but we will most certainly do them differently. Imagine what would the world look and be like if we were all the same, doing the same things. The picture I have in my mind as I am imagining this is not looking good, diversity is key. This is one of the reasons I think God created a man and woman, they are supposed to serve different purposes.

We have to practice being ourselves and be proud of our distinctiveness. Strive to be yourself and never imitate others. Learn from them but never imitate them for you will only become a good copy; destroying your unique power to serve your purpose.

Proverbs 29:18 in the King James Version reads "where there is no vision, people perish: but he that keepeth the law, happy is he."

Those with a clear vision, live a narrow life, life with less distractions and frustrations. Your focus gets directed to very few specific tasks to perform, in turn your worries and stress level drops massively.

Vision controls your choices, the moment you know where you are heading, by default you will also know what roads won't take you there. Similarly, the moment you know what you must do, you will automatically know what you must not do. Vision gives you the address to your destination.

Vision creates discipline, people believe and admire those who are disciplined. If someone offers you something that is not aligned with your purpose and vision, it is easy to reject the offer. Without vision it is very difficult to refuse anything and that will complicate your life. A complicated life has got no joy and certainly no peace.

VISION AND FOCUS

We were not born to do everything; the truth is: only few things matter. You may have heard successful people saying these words, "This one thing that I do." Their focus goes to this one thing. Anthony Robbins says, "Energy flows where focus is." The reason why most people get confused and distracted is because they try to have a hand in everything and in the process, they consume their energy and as a result confusion and distraction creep in.

The sooner you define your life purpose and have a clear vision, the sooner you will use your remaining years in this world wisely and effectively. If you are like me and you are already over forty years old, then there is no more time to experiment. Living life purposefully by having a clear vision, causes you to succeed in all your goals sooner. This in turn will make you find joy and inner peace. It is therefore very important that you review, analyze and amend your life purpose.

"There can be no greater gift than that of giving one's time and energy to helping others without expecting anything in return" by Nelson Mandela.

Some Key Points To Remember

LIFE WITHOUT PURPOSE	LIFE WITH PURPOSE
Live for survival Troubled by little issues and life challenges Full of worry Prone to frustration Stressful and tough type of living Emotionally unstable Confused life and out of focus Always feeling overwhelmed Easily influenced Weak mental strength	Feeling in control and in-charge of own life Fewer worries Control over worry and fear Clear choices and not easily influenced Easy decision making Always calm and in peace Joyful, happy and stable life High success rate in most minor to major goals Simple straight forward life Improved energy and focus

My Personal Notes

_____

_____

_____

_____

_____

_____

_____

"

Purpose and vision are the source of discipline and motivation. A life of discipline creates trust and trust creates joy and inner peace

Pheello Ntuka

CHAPTER 2

Learn How to Detach and Let Go

The issue of feeling attached to the material things of this world is very broad. In this chapter we will focus mainly on the basics of finding inner peace when you feel more like you are trapped or you are simply afraid of losing anything you might think valuable to you.

Have you ever felt like you are caged and could not find ways to escape? Have you ever felt like you are about to lose something valuable to you or perhaps someone you love dearly? We have all experienced these kinds of mixed feelings in the course of our lives. When you are over attached and perhaps entangled to anything, your chances of having inner peace are very slim. It is important to learn how to detach and free yourself so you can have inner peace. Detaching means letting go of whatever you are emotionally attached to, this could be little things such as your jewelry, clothes, electronic devices, to bigger things like your cars, property and people you love.

Detaching does not mean you don't care, but it means separating self-worth from physical possessions so you can find peace within.

Nothing is permanent in this world, and the sooner we learn and understand this, the sooner we will find peace and live happily. When we are born, we come to this world with nothing in our hands, and we are going to leave this world the same way.

How can you find peace when you think owning everything will lead to contentment? The moment you realize you are about to lose it all, your stress level will probably skyrocket, and you will surely feel unhappy. It hurts to let go, but it hurts even more to hold on. There are lot of things in our lives that are beyond our control, the only power we have is control of our emotions and our thinking. It is very important to take control of your own life and be in control of how you think, feel and behave. This can help you find inner-peace. I believe doing this will free you from being attached and entangled by the forces of this world.

Remember that you can do absolutely anything but not everything. Energy flows where your focus is, if for some reason you want ownership of everything in this world, you confuse the energy flow. You also confuse yourself by trying to get your hands on everything which is not really possible. This will lead to unhappiness and eventually steal your inner peace.

The day I grasped this basic principle, my focus changed from being all over the place to a specific goal, one thing at the time. That also gave me joy, inner peace and happiness. I have found the below points to be very useful when feeling emotionally attached to someone or something.

Sad but true that trying to own a person, being your child, spouse or anyone, will cause you more pain that joy.

Over-possessiveness could lead to obsession which could also result in greediness.

DAILY HAPPENINGS

We all experience different challenges in our daily lives both good and bad. Most of these challenges are beyond our control.

It is not what happens that determine our success, but what we do about these challenges. Someone might for instance experience a tough setback, say losing all of his money at the bank due to fraud or bad consumer debts and decide to

33

commit suicide. Another may decide to build their wealth all over again. Same incident but different ways of handling them.

Detaching and letting go of the world's material objects and freeing yourself from negative emotions will increase your level of happiness and make you find inner peace. There is a technique that I use a lot and has helped me to free myself every time I face a negative emotion and is simply called "Emotional Freedom Technique." This is simply telling yourself that no matter the situation you may be facing at that particular time, "You still love yourself and that you forgive yourself", as simple as it may sound, this technique has helped me overcome many negative emotions I encountered.

GENEROSITY AND COMPASSION IN ACTION

Life is precious, the fact that you are still alive today means you are blessed already, the rest comes after and I believe we must all be grateful for this. If we were to choose just one thing in the world, I am positive that we would all choose life, for when you are alive you can build up whatever you want.

When you are no longer attached to any material objects or anyone for that matter, you can easily give to others.

When you are generous, you give without expecting anything in return. The universe will also be generous to you, giving away your material objects to those who need them more than you, is a good sign of kindness and love. Here is my favorite quote by *Anthony Robbins*" *"The secret to receiving is giving"*

It is not easy to give or provide what you don't have, to give love you must first have love. This is one of the reasons why many relationships fail, trying to give someone love when you are still not sure if you love yourself or not. You can love more when you are attached to nothing, when your mind and emotions are free and calm. The same applies to appreciation, excitement and cheerfulness, you first have to show and feel these positive emotions before you can start sharing them with others. Imagine an angry fearful comedian trying to make people laugh, I don't think that would work so well, don't you?

THE POWER OF FORGIVENESS

The word forgive is one of the words I believe is extremely difficult for human beings to say and mean. Its definition in simple terms means "to intentionally decide to release any feelings of anger or revenge toward a person or a group who may have harmed you in any manner and make peace with the situation or the person." Learning and practicing the process of letting go of your negative feelings through the process of forgiveness is one critical tool you may use which will guarantee you joy and inner peace.

The greatest human goal is the ability to maintain inner-peace in every situation. Among the greatest obstacles to inner peace are anger, blame and other negative emotions. If these feelings are not being taken care of, they may lead to serious hatred, regrets, inner-conflict, suicide and acts of violence. In order to totally eliminate these negative feelings, as hard as it may be, the only way to help yourself maintain your joy and inner peace is by learning and practicing forgiveness and let go of these feelings. *Courageous people do not fear forgiving, for the sake of peace" by Nelson Mandela.*

I am still a student and in the process of learning the word of God for I believe in continuous learning. One of the major lessons we find in the Lord's Prayer in the book of life is that *"we must forgive those who sinned against us if we want our sins to be forgiven as well"* (Matthew 6:12). It is always amazing how we want good things to happen to us but not willing to do the same for others. When you forgive others, you do it mainly to free yourself and not the other person. This is one of the reasons why there is power in forgiveness. You are not necessarily doing the other person a favour, but you do it to free yourself from all negative feelings you may have at that moment. Your major goal here is to totally free yourself.

If you are really serious about changing your life, changing to the path to light, the life full of joy and inner peace. It is very important that you learn and practice letting go of your past errors and forgive yourself for anything you cannot change. We hold the keys and the power to change our stories and the meaning they may represent. In my own experience and that of others, the following are usually four people you must forgive.

Yourself.

When you forgive yourself you free yourself from all negative feelings. You create yet another opportunity to start all over again and move on, this time with a better experience.

_____

_____

_____

_____

_____

_____

_____

_____

Your parents.

Forgive your parents, living or dead, be grateful for they gave you life, which is priceless. If you are happy to be alive, everything else is a bonus, if you lose your life, nothing else matter.

_____

_____

_____

_____

_____

_____

_____

_____

Your ex.

In any relationship, there is always two people involved, which means you partially contributed to the failure of that relationship and therefore you were also responsible. It is therefore necessary to focus on what you did than what you are blaming the other person for, be responsible for your actions

_____

_____

_____

_____

Everyone else.

Some people may not fall in the first three categories. Free yourself of the unnecessary excess baggage that comes from holding onto offence. Forgive friends, relatives and others who may have hurt you.

_____

_____

_____

_____

The art of forgiving is the ability to emotionally *"letting it go."* Most pains come from other people and external influences, unless you are physically sick. It really does not make sense to spend your time and life miserable, angry and blaming someone who is out there enjoying himself and having a good time and frankly doesn't even think or care about you. Unforgiveness literally eats you up and tortures your soul and therefore steals your joy and inner peace. The seeds of unforgiveness are guaranteed to bear sour and bitter fruits.

Some Key Points To Remember

Be open to everything but attached to nothing.

You can do anything but not everything.

The pie is big enough for us all, only pick your portion and let go of others.

Over-possessiveness could lead to obsession which could also result in greediness.

Learn how to detach and let go of the world's material objects.

Generosity is one of the keys to joy and inner peace.

The secret to receiving is giving. There is real power in forgiveness.

Let go of your past mistakes, detach yourself from negative feelings.

Letting go and forgiving others for the pain they may have caused you is the best recipe to release anger.

My Personal Notes

_____

_____

_____

_____

_____

_____

_____

_____

66

Learning and practicing the power of
"forgiveness and letting go" of the
world's material things including
human beings, will guarantee
you a life full of joy and inner peace,
life without fear of losing anything.

Pheello Ntuka

CHAPTER 3

How Grateful Are You?

In 2006 my wife and I went through a rough time in our marriage. It was so bad that I made a choice to temporarily leave our home for almost three months. I remember we were expecting our second born, it was more like our love was being tested by the evil forces of life. We would argue over almost every little thing and the bad influence was also taking its toll. All the advice we were getting seemed to separate us further.

Our love was decreasing every day, she was still looking for a job and I must admit our finances were also contributing to our failing marriage. I was working as a level one network operator and it was very difficult to keep up with our lifestyle. As the saying goes, *"The first five years of every marriage are the most difficult part of this wonderful process."*

We were really going through the storm and did not know how to change towards the path that will make us go around this storm and not through it. We were in a season of winter in marriage. This was a very disturbing and hurtful experience that caused severe emotional pain for both of us. We were not prepared to take the blame or responsibility for our actions and kept blaming each other. The relations between our parents and both side of the in-laws were also getting affected. No parents want to see their children in tears and heart broken. I am still learning the book of life, but I do recall Adam blaming Eve for not abiding by God's law. Adam blamed Eve and said, *"It is the woman You gave me that made me commit this offence" (Gen 3).* It was also easy for me to put the blame on the woman whom I strongly believed God chose to be my wife.

Perhaps you are already asking what all this has to do with being grateful, and I want to assure you it has to do with everything. The word "Grateful" means showing great appreciation for something received or done, being thankful for what you already have, no matter how small or big it can be. Later that year I managed to swallow my pride and overpower my ego and started to listen to my heart. I am still enjoying the benefits of swallowing my pride and shutting down my ego. Today I am still very grateful that I married this amazing woman who showed me unconditional love since day one.

We sometime get taken up by our ego and end up being blinded by the external forces of life and eventually lose all the precious gifts from God. I have learnt that it is not possible to be happy without first being grateful, "there is no happiness without gratitude." You cannot have inner peace if you still have unresolved issues in your life or are still stuck in the past. It is important that we learn to be happy with what we have and not delay our happiness for some event that is supposed to happen in the future. Gratitude overpowers fear and sadness.

PEACE AGAINST COMPLAINING

Having inner peace means your mind is in harmony with your emotions, meaning there is no internal war. The moment you start complaining about something, you automatically drop your level of happiness which in return takes away your peace. I know a lot of people who are affected by nonstop complaints. This usually starts small and eventually grows to become a habit. I am sure you can relate to those kinds of people who complain about every little thing, they have the ability to find mistakes in everything they see, touch, smell or taste. These are the people whom I believe suffer from the "Ungratefulness Syndrome." I have a colleague who is a good example of this type of person. When he looks outside through the window, he does not see the sunshine and the beautiful garden, instead he sees the little dirt and small marks of paint on the window. He does not try to figure out what is right, but he is constantly figuring out what is wrong and gets delighted when he finds errors.

Lack of gratitude is one of the biggest blessing blockers. The moment you become grateful; you open up more channels to receive more. Lack of gratitude causes all the blessings that could come your way to be blocked. This really makes sense and applies to every area of our lives, if we don't appreciate and become grateful for what we already have we may lose it.

Most people complain about the few things they have. They would complain about the only thing they have without having a backup plan should they lose it. This is a sign of being ungrateful. Gratitude is the healthiest emotion of all, it is not possible to be angry and grateful simultaneously, you cannot be fearful and grateful all at once. Gratefulness is like a reset button to all sorts of emotional imbalances and therefore a key to unlocking joy and inner-peace.

I have seen lot of people who make a lot of money and hold key positions or own businesses but are still not happy and have no inner-peace. Our parliament is full of ministers whom I think are making fortunes, but they are still not happy. When you are ungrateful, you become greedy which leads to being empty inside. In our churches, people pray and worship the lord weekly but still have no peace within. This comes to the realization that happiness does not come from the material things.

Having lot of flashy toys, sports cars and perhaps a three storey house does not necessarily bring inner peace and joy to your life but could bring short term gratification which can be gone the next day. If you are thankful and appreciate the little things you already have, you open up more channels to receive even more. There is a phrase I like that says: "Where there is appreciation and gratitude, there is duplication." You cannot push and pull simultaneously, if you push something away and at the same time try to attract it, you are simply confusing the law of attraction - you attract more of your most dominant thoughts, good or bad, positive or negative.

PAST VS FUTURE

When I started working in 1998, I was happy that I was getting a salary and I could buy myself some nice clothes and decent food. I remember I was very excited when I received that long-awaited call. My parents and my younger sister were all happy that our standard of living was now going to improve. I got very excited when I was told that I was going to earn R33000 per annum, which then to me was a lot of money. It was enough for someone without many responsibilities. I was unaware that the world of money and finances needed some basic skills for one to live better and enjoy the rewards that come with money.

For many years I was just comfortable with my earnings for I could still provide my family with all their basic needs. Years went by and I started experiencing serious money challenges which led to me becoming dishonest. I would constantly break promises to my family. I am sure we all know when you reach that stage where the money ends before the month. My expenses were suddenly far higher than my income and I found myself drowned by debt. This experience got me so frustrated I started blaming my employer. I started blaming the economy, racism, the fuel price, the company policy and almost everything. In my mind it meant I was no longer making enough money and was always hoping for that annual increase which is usually not guaranteed. I was blaming all I have, I thought of studying further hoping that I will perhaps get promoted and earn better than I was earning. You see I was actually missing the point, and that showed a sign of not being grateful for what I already had. I know lot of people who are going through the same unpleasant experience.

Through personal development I discovered that for me to get the situation under control and improve my finances, I had to increase my financial education and refine my life philosophy in relation to money. The knowledge that I accumulated improved my finances drastically. Our past can serve us well if we learn from it and become grateful for the experiences instead of beating ourselves up every time we think about our past mistakes. We have to appreciate and be thankful for our past mistakes and learn from them so we can reduce the possibility of committing the same errors in the future.

Note that the greatest threat to your future is your past. One of the secrets to finding inner-peace is to "make peace" with your past mistakes and find ways to learn from them. Old knowledge must never limit new knowledge, and most people allow their lives to remain in the past which limits them from progressing into the future. You cannot erase your past, but you can learn from it. The moment you decide to move on, you also open up your mind to new possibilities and opportunities. If you are trapped by your past failures, you block all the other things you could do in future. Do not allow your memory to immobilize you, for this will certainly steal your joy and inner peace, this results in your major and minor goals being unsuccessful.

The past is dangerous if it is not serving you, the greatest thing you can do is learn to let go of your past failures and use them as feedback. The key is to learn from those experiences, take whatever was important, and move your focus to something more significant today. The moment you start the process of accepting that no one is perfect and that you are human, the sooner you will regain your inner peace. Again, I am a novice when coming to the bible, but I do believe that it is the most important book on the planet. I also believe God forgives our sins and past life errors. The key is to make sure you learn from your past life errors, so you do not take them with into the future. A repeated mistake will certainly paralyze your future, as the genius Albert Einstein said, *"Insanity is doing the same thing over and over and expecting different results."*

_____

_____

_____

_____

_____

_____

_____

_____

Below are just few examples of the most ignored but really significant elements of life to be grateful for:

- Your Source (The Creator Himself)

- Your life

- The sunlight

- The oxygen we breath

- Day and Night

- Seasons of the year

- Time

- Our God given five senses

- The soil and the rain

- The seeds

- Our relationships with others

- Your temple of God (Your own body)

- The Goldmine between our ears (The Brain)

- The Soul (Feelings, Willpower, Mind)

- Natural Surroundings – Environment (land, plants, animals, forests etc.)

Life is a journey that is full of stop stations and humps to slow us down when we over-run the laws of life. We have to be grateful in each stop station so we can move forward and enter the future. This precious journey seems to pause in times of sorrow, grief, sickness, sadness, financial crises, misery, shame, humiliation, anger, depression etc. Each stop station is teaching us something we need to know and is preparing us for the final destination. Some stop stations are better than others, some stations will have enough food, water, money, love, happiness, and better jobs than others. We have to be grateful in all these stations so we can find peace within. The principle of becoming grateful for all the little things is one of the master keys to finding joy and inner peace. "The root of joy is gratefulness" by David Steindl-Rast.

Some Key Points To Remember

Gratitude overpowers fear and sadness.

One of the keys to inner peace is having the ability to overpower your own ego and pride simply by being grateful of the little you already have.

Gratefulness means your mind is in harmony with your emotions which gives you inner peace.

Lack of gratitude blocks away all your possible opportunities and your blessings.

Gratitude is the healthiest emotion.

It not possible to be fearful and grateful at the same time.

The most ignored but very important element of life to be grateful for is your own life and its source (Your creator)

Be grateful for your job and your source of income for if wisely used, could be your only vehicle to your dreams and your future success.

Be grateful for the little things you already accumulated for this is one of the master keys to success, joy and inner peace.

Gratefulness is one best medicine that is capable of neutralizing all negative feelings.

My Personal Notes

_____

_____

_____

_____

_____

"

"Gratefulness is a great
antidote that neutralizes the intensity
of all negative emotions, the lower
the intensity of negative emotions,
the higher the level of inner peace
you will receive."

Pheello Ntuka

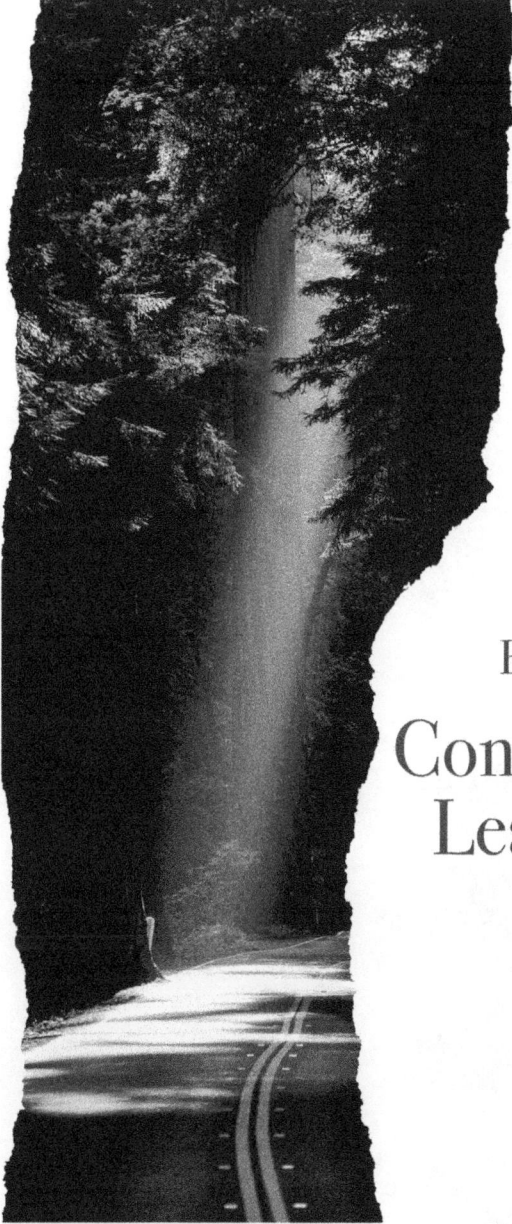

PART 2

Continuous Learning

CHAPTER 4

Food for the Mind

―――――――――――

There is a phrase that I have learnt few years back and wished I could have known it while I was still at tertiary level. The phrase made me realize that sometimes you think you know enough until you face a real-life challenge. The phrase is, "Being in an unconscious incompetent state of mind", which simply means, not knowing or not being aware that you don't know.

It could be something important that you should have known before, and you later realize that it is actually affecting your current results or your life in general.

There are four stages of learning that I found to be significant for me to explain in this chapter. I use these phrases a lot when I conduct trainings and are now part of my vocabulary, here are the four stages of learning.

UNCONSCIOUS INCOMPETENCE

This is a state of not knowing or not being aware that you do not know what you supposed to know.

In most working environment you find people have been working in one field performing the same function for over 10 years and assume that they have 10 years' experience.

There is a difference between doing the same thing repeated for 10 years and working for 10 years in different fields building various skills, knowledge and experience.

Many times, in an interview, most people only realize then that they were not aware they had limited knowledge and skills.

CONSCIOUS INCOMPETENCE

This is a state where you know and are aware that you lack a specific skill or knowledge and you are planning to do something about it. In an example of someone who wants to learn how to drive a car, it is in this state of learning where you are fully aware and know that you cannot drive a car.

CONSCIOUS COMPETENCE

This third state is when you are now learning the skill, but you have to be fully focused on every little activity.

In our above example of a new driver, when you sit on the driver's seat you have to think when turning the steering and changing the gears and you probably look down on the pedals, no car radio should be switched on for it will disrupt your concentration.

UNCONSCIOUS COMPETENCE

This final state is when you know the skill by heart, you can now perform the skill without thinking and with your eyes closed, you are now on "autopilot mode."

In our previous example, you can change gears and turn the steering wheel while enjoying a cup of coffee, not a good thing to do though, you are now simply the master in your field. In a world of soccer, you become a "key player."

I have discovered that the best recipe for growth and development is to become unconsciously competent in your field or in your job. You can achieve massive growth by becoming the master at what you do and in your own territory. This is the level where your knowledge and level of competence is automatic, you can do what you do with your eyes closed. We are all affected by what we know and what we do not know. A quote by Albert Einstein says: "Once you stop learning, you start dying"

When I first attended an interview in 1996 at Vaal Triangle Technikon, now known as Vaal University of Technology. I remember I was in a class and the lecturer was teaching on electronic applications suddenly decided to call my name. I was randomly chosen from other students that got higher marks from the previous semester test.

He then explained to me that there are gentlemen from Sasol looking for students that are performing well in this subject. He then gave me the room number where I would find these gentlemen. As I entered the room, I saw three white gentlemen wearing suits and ties looking very intimidating. They did not waste time and started throwing questions at me.

First, my English was very poor I could not even answer the most popular interview question "Tell us about yourself." It was very hard for me to construct a simple English sentence, let alone a paragraph, and bear in mind that I was already in my third year in tertiary education. I learnt that I had prioritised listening and writing English language over speaking it and that was my undoing. This experience took away my self-esteem and massively dropped my self-confidence. I had never felt so embarrassed in my entire life till that point and did not want to share this with anyone.

All along I was under the impression that I was the clever one, I thought I knew it all. I questioned myself for many years after this experience and could not find answers. I wanted to know if there was anything wrong with me or if our then educational system was at the highest level compared to the private schools. The incident made me scared of speaking English especially in places full of people I was not familiar with.

The mind is like an operating system of a computer, like Windows Seven or any other operating system, it needs some software to be loaded so it can function properly and run certain programs. All our experiences, the things we have been hearing and observing from our childhood are stored in our minds, this data or information can either serve you or work against you consciously or unconsciously. There is a book that I highly recommend by Joseph Murphy: "The Power of Your Subconscious Mind: Prentice-Hall Inc, 1963" which explains the mind in more details.

It is absolutely important to pour only ingredients that are good for your mind and your development.

EMPOWERING YOUR MIND

The mind is not the brain; the brain is an organ that stores the mind. The mind is divided into two parts, the conscious and sub-conscious mind. The conscious mind is the portion that analyses and tries to find logic in everything. On the other side, the subconscious mind works based on your previous programs or past events, values and habits. When you are unconscious, it is the subconscious mind that takes over and controls your life, for an example, when you are asleep, you can still breathe and move your body.

It is very important to always be aware of what you feed your mind, for this is how you program your mind. From little things such as the type of news you listen to, the things you observe every day, either by listening to the radio or watching television. Whatever you feed your mind becomes your knowledge and creates certain programs in your mind which then determine how you behave. The quality and quantity of your knowledge determines the quality of your life and the results you get in your life. The amount of money we are currently earning is mainly due to the level of knowledge we have. The less knowledge you have in your field of work, the less chances of you to climb up the ladder. The opposite is also true, the more knowledge you have on a particular subject or in your field, the more experience you build which then makes you the master or the specialist in that field.

When you master your field and somehow an opportunity arises for a promotion, it finds you fully ready and that is how most people grow. If you are not growing, you are dying.

As human beings, we are affected by what we know, the more you know about health and great lifestyle, the better and longer you can live. The more knowledge you have about your finances, the more money you can make and faster. The more knowledge you have on relationships or marriage, the greater understanding and stable relationship you'll have, and you will possibly make better choices in your relationship.

If you have a specific purpose in your life and know exactly what you want and which path you are taking. This will make you to focus on specific lessons aligned with this purpose which in turn will make you become competent in your field. This will eliminate anything that is not helping you to grow and achieve your goals. The main challenge is that we are always surrounded by misleading and toxic information, which can easily influence us badly and limit us from finding joy and inner peace. Insufficient knowledge whether due to ignorance or laziness could be deadly and it will sooner or later affect your future.

My first horrible interview made me wake up and start questioning myself about my level of knowledge and understanding. I wanted to know all possible reasons why others were getting those bursaries and great jobs. Have you ever wondered why one person keeps on getting promoted while you are stuck in one position for many years? The better questions to ask yourself are the following:

- How is your level of knowledge with regards to that particular subject or the career you are following?

- Are you more skilled and experienced than any of your competitors or colleagues in the same field?

- Are you willing to do more than you are paid for and willing to do the things others are not willing to do?

- Are you constantly improving your knowledge and skills every day? And if not, what is stopping you?

- How do you spend most of your time?

- What and who are your sources of your information?

- And lastly, who do you spend most of your time with?

- What are you learning from these people?

We now live in a world of technology where information is right at your fingertips. With access to internet, Google and YouTube, we have libraries in almost every suburb and townships, so finding the relevant information related to your goal or dream is no longer a problem like before. The big question is what do you really do with all the access to information? Are you using it to serve you and gain more knowledge or to work against your goals?

GOLD MINE BETWEEN YOUR EARS

When I started to feed my mind with only positive relevant information that is in harmony with my life purpose, I started to make better choices and my life radically improved. I am happier and at peace now. I can now easily tell when I am receiving improper and misleading information which is not aligned to my major goals. You have to be very selective and careful about what you listen to, the books you read and the people you surround yourself with all affect you and can lead you to either failure or success.

It is a great challenge to know almost everything in this world. It is, however, very important to know more about your field of work or career, your interests and your purpose. It is also very critical to learn more and become the master in your own field. If you want more money, learn more about money, if want happiness, study happiness, same if you want to be healthy, study health and keep on increasing your knowledge on that particular subject.

It won't make sense that you want to improve your marriage but you spent most of your time with your friends, similarly if you want to get a promotion but you don't focus on learning more and improving your value in your specific career, it is like baking cakes with cement instead of using flour.

Feed your mind with ONLY good ingredients and season with relevant "spices", which will help you to achieve your dreams and goals quicker. John Earl Shoaff says: "We want to be like farmers. We are going to plant seeds, and these seeds that we plant are the seeds we are going to reap". We all have the gold mine which is situated between our ears and was given to us free of charge. Why not use this mine which is our mental factory by planting only invaluable information?

THOUGHTS HAVE POWER

One of the major principles of living a life full of joy and inner peace is having the skills to monitor your thoughts. Our minds generate many thoughts every day, these thoughts can either make or break you. Our lives are run by the laws of the universe, the law of attraction states that what we constantly think about manifests. We are where we are today because of our past thoughts, therefore it is vital that we pour good and positive ingredients into our mental factory. The ingredients that will build our future and that of our children.

When I understood this principle, I could not wait to start applying it. Before consuming any information, I ask if it will help me achieve my major goals and lead me to finding joy and inner peace?

The importance of monitoring your thoughts is very critical. You really have to be careful what you think about every now and then for this affects your emotions. If you think about something horrible that has happened to you 10 years back, you suddenly feel sad and becomes very emotional. You then listen to your favorite song which reminds you of an event you attended or your happiest moment, your emotions suddenly change from sadness to joy.

This leads us to another aspect of monitoring your thoughts and it is known as self-conversation or "self-talk." We all talk to ourselves every each and every second, this internal conversation can build or destroy us, and is so powerful it can lead you to unhappiness. You really want to be in control of your self-talk. That little voice talking to you all the time can easily mislead you if it is not controlled and redirected to focus only on your life purpose, vision or your goals.

It is wise to constantly redirect your thoughts towards your goals. How you feel now is a sign of whether you are thinking positive or negative thoughts. If you constantly become aware of what you are feeling, good or bad, then you can quickly change your thinking which will in turn change that specific self-talk and your mood will also change. This principle is related to another chapter which we will discuss later in this book.

The key principle here is first, feed your mind with empowering information by constantly loading your mental factory with information that is aligned with your life purpose, vision and your goals. Second, monitor your thoughts and your self-conversation by constantly monitoring your feelings. This will certainly need some practice until it becomes a habit. This principle will counter any negative thoughts and self-limitations you might have, and you will have peace and become a happier person. *"You either control your mind, or it controls you"- by Napoleon Hill.*

Some Key Points To Remember

Your mind needs a lot of good food (Best information) Pour only the best ingredients into your mental factory.

Empower your mind and filter out negative information that may steal your joy.

Constantly improve your level of knowledge and experience. Be the best in your own field and master your skills or talents.

Thoughts are very powerful for they affect your feelings.

Monitor your own "self-talk."

If you are not growing, you are dying.

Become unconscious competent at what you do and be the CEO of your own life.

Your mental factory is bound to produce fruits, sweet or sour.

My Personal Notes

_____

_____

_____

_____

_____

_____

_____

_____

_____

66

"The ingredients that you pour into your mental factory are bound to produce fruits - sweet or sour. Be careful what you put into your mental factory."

Pheello Ntuka

CHAPTER 5

Today's Habits Affect Your Tomorrow

On the 25th of March 2019, my father passed on after a short illness, we later discovered that it was actually a long illness known only by one of his close friend. We found out about his illness about two weeks before his last day on this earth. My father had a habit of keeping things to himself, he was a man of very few words. My belief is that, had he disclosed his illness to one of the family members earlier, he would have gotten some help in time. Habits are the little acts we do repeatedly and over time they become part of us. A habit can be defined as a practice that one does regularly and sometimes without knowing it or realizing that it is being done. It is said that an act repeated for about thirty to sixty days will form a habit. We all have good and bad habits that we perform daily. Your bad habit can create a serious dent in your life and your productivity. We all know people in our working environment, who perform poorly simply because they have in the past developed negative habits. They spend too much time chit-chatting when they supposed to be working, taking too many smoke breaks just to avoid doing what they should be doing.

I have in my life observed people close to me spending over eight hours every day just watching television and always asking for money, always complaining how difficult life is. I am sure you also have someone you know like this. My questions to them is that, why don't they convert at least half of this time into learning new skills which will eventually turn into an asset to generate income? It is very easy to develop a habit of wasting time and procrastinating. Most toxic habits are formed by just following the crowd. The moment you realize that whatever you are doing is done by most people, this may be a good time to stop and ask yourself why you are also doing it and also if you should be doing it.

Most acts that are not adding any value are easy to do, on the other hand, the activities that add value are not so easy to do. It is easy just to sit and watch your favourite TV program when others are learning and improving themselves. It is also not easy to pick up that educational book and read. It also not easy to stand up from that comfortable couch and go do some work.

My current function gave me an opportunity to conduct "Performance and Development Management." This where I learnt that most people do not perform to their highest level due to two main reasons. The first one is a lack of interest in what they do because there is not much growth and development. The second one is being in one area of work for many years doing the same function. This no engagement, leading them to developing a habit of just going through the day and not getting something out of the day. Most people want to earn money, but they do not really want to work for it. It is easy to enjoy spending that money but not easy to work for it. I have learned that when you do something of your highest interest and value, you really don't need motivation to do it. Assess whether what you are currently working on or doing is of your highest or low interest and value? You could be spending too much time creating habits of low interest and value.

In one of the previous chapters we touched on the subject of how the little things count more. The other side of this coin is that the little acts performed repeatedly over time create habits good or bad. It is therefore important to monitor your seemingly insignificant daily acts, for ignoring this fact could severely affect your future. Our habits today determine our path to failure or success. This is the major reason why habits are so important and need to be constantly monitored and when necessary, refined.

If you do not take care of this and neglect your daily acts, they will surely steal your inner peace. Your current status in life is due, in part, to your daily habits, what do you do from the moment you wake up?

Here is one of the major lessons about habits, "EVERYTHING AFFECTS EVERYTHING." One habit of neglect leads to another, then it eventually decreases our self-worth, our self-esteem and our self-confidence. If you neglect having an apple a day, you will surely ignore walking around the block, you will then neglect reading a book and lose out on increasing your knowledge, soon or later your bank account will be empty and you will later wish you had extra time in this world.

DEVELOP AND PRACTICE THE HABITS OF WINNERS

What separates the best from the rest comes down to habits. A few good habits is really all it takes. Two, three or more will become even better and make a massive difference in your life, career and the people around you. Your habits will determine how close or how far you are from your major goals and vision. It is therefore very significant to align your good habits and your daily actions to your life purpose and of course your vision. Some of the habits of winners include, but are not limited to:

- Getting up early and planning your day

- Putting your relationship with your loved ones first

- Regarding others more than themselves

- Under-promising but over-delivering

- Always give others more than they expect

- Becoming a passionate learner and a good student

- Becoming the best at what you do and interested in others opinion

- Welcoming any constructive criticism

- Becoming open to everything but attached to nothing

- Using your time wisely and efficiently

- Practice forgiveness, you are doing it for your own good and this will guarantee you inner peace.

THE VALUE OF GOOD HABITS OVER BAD HABITS

Practice forgiveness, you are doing it for your own good and this will guarantee you inner peace.

The great value of a good habit is that you don't have to think about it, the act becomes automatic to you. If you repeatedly do something good or learn a new skill, after a while you end up doing it unconsciously, you become unconsciously competent. Practice a good habit long enough to make it yours and own it. Everything worth doing is an uphill task and that is a fact, I have never heard someone talking about accidental achievement. To get to the top of the mountain you have to walk all the way up, no one will lift you up there, there are no elevators.

You have to put effort to achieve all your goals, here is the key phrase: *"Inspiration does a lot better when it is coupled with perspiration."* Do the work and you will get inspired, do not wait until you get inspired to do the work.

Our current habits do affect our future and the results we are currently getting in our lives. If you are not happy with your current results. One of the places to look at are your habits, make a list of all your daily activities and check where you spent most of your time and what exactly do you do most of the time. The second part is to check if your activities are in line with your goals, and if not, perhaps it is time to refine your habits. Develop the habits of winners so you can find inner peace. It is not possible to find peace within when your habits are working against you. Successful people develop habits that help them grow. Choose your habits wisely.

Bad habits on the other hand are part of our lives, it is therefore important to take note of them and learn from their negative experiences. Life has negative moments and it necessary to learn how to handle the negatives. We should not ignore the negative habits but develop the skills to learn from them. Bad habits are like weeds that grow in the garden, if they are being ignored, they will soon take over the garden. Weeds grow automatically in every garden; we have to make sure we take good care of our garden. The rule from our Creator is six days of labour and only one day of rest, I am sure he had a very good reason for this, which I suppose is, if we take too much time on break, then the weeds will take over the garden.

There is a great war between good and bad habits. If "Good" sleeps, "Evil" takes over, the absence of light will result in darkness. We have to make sure the "GOOD HABITS" are always fully awake, otherwise bad habits will take over. This could lead into an unproductive, lazy and misguided society. Your habits do affect your joy and inner-peace, it is really significant to review and amend your habits to your advantage. A quote by Warren Buffet says: *"Chains of habit are too light to be felt until they are too heavy to be broken"*.

_____

_____

_____

_____

_____

_____

_____

_____

_____

_____

_____

_____

_____

_____

_____

_____

_____

_____

_____

_____

_____

Some Key Points To Remember

Today's habits affect your future. Everything affects everything.

Be careful not to develop a habit of neglecting your own life philosophy.

Practice the habits of winners.

Habits help us create an automatic life pattern of specific actions, practice good habits.

There is great value in good habits over bad ones.

Bad habits are like the weeds in the garden, if ignored they will soon take over the garden.

A week of neglect could cause a year of repairs.

Our habits today determine our path to success or failure.

The little acts performed repeatedly over time form habits, good or bad.

My Personal Notes

_____

_____

_____

_____

_____

_____

_____

_____

_____

"

"A week of neglect could cause a year of repairs, this is simply called the disorder of bad habits, be aware, today's habits affect your future."
Pheello Ntuka

CHAPTER 6

The Power of Choices

The subject of choices is very broad and unlimited; we have to make choices in our daily lives. Some are simple while others can be tough, some may be small while others are big. For a decision to be made, one will first have to make a choice, for there is usually more than one option to choose from. The complexity of making a choice is that, most of the time one might not be certain whether the choice made is a good one or a bad one.

Have you ever found yourself looking for a specific destination with no map or an electronic device to give you the correct direction, and suddenly you reach a T-Junction where you are forced to either turn left or right? I am sure we can all relate to this scenario. Somehow in our lives we reach a point where we have to make that kind of a choice, whether you want to or not. Making a choice can be the most difficult thing to do when you are aware that it will affect your future. The choices we make today will certainly determine our future and could lead us into an unknown or known destination. It is therefore necessary to find new ways and better options to help us make smart choices so that we make better decisions. In this chapter we will look at some of the important principles we need to learn when we have to make those tough choices, choices that will lead us onto the bridge to finding peace and happiness.

THE WAR IS ON

We all fight for one of two things, first is that we all do what we can to avoid pain, and second we do things in order to find pleasure. Each person in this world is primarily concerned with his or her own agenda and wants only positive results. This is one of the reasons why we get stressed and feel down when life starts to throw unexpected negative situations on us.

I have learnt how to deal with every negative situation I come across in my daily life. Life is both positive and negative, therefore we need to prepare ourselves for all the challenges we might face. No one ever said life was going to be easy, this is one of many reasons I believe God created us differently from any other thing on planet earth. The only major difference between human beings and other animals is the "goldmine between our ears" - the mind. This is one gift of life that we all possess, and was given to us free of charge, for with it we can train ourselves to make better and wiser choices. We have the capabilities of choosing between love and hate, health and sickness, anger and happiness, life or death, ego or acceptance, fear or curiosity, pride or willingness, the list is endless.

A good principle of happiness and inner peace, and that is everything starts as a thought, and this thought whether positive or negative will immediately create an emotion related to that thought and that emotion will then make you behave in a certain way. I have over the years practiced how to monitor my thinking, by being aware of my thoughts. With this, I can also monitor my emotions. The moment you change your thinking you immediately experience a different emotion, whether positive or negative. We will discuss this in more details in the following chapters.

The war is on within our minds, emotions and bodies, it is very difficult for anyone to find happiness and inner peace when you are unable to win your inner fights. We all have this inner conflict which in turn affects our choices, and in the end affects our decisions. This can be from little things such as choosing between two items or brands in your local store to perhaps a more complex situation such as to continue to be involved in an unpleasant relationship hoping things will be better someday or move on and look for a more pleasant one. I have experienced lots of internal fights in my life and I still do.

What seems to work better for me in making the right choice is asking myself if the choice I am about to make will still feel good even after a week, a month and a year. I have since learnt that a good choice is the one you won't regret in the future. It is therefore important and necessary to ask yourself what are the chances of you regretting making this choice in few days, weeks, months or after a year. I have learnt my lesson after buying a reliable car and later decide to sell it for another one with lot of mechanical problems. This is just one of many examples of making a choice that you may later regret.

INTELLIGENT MENTAL PREPARATION (IMP) PRINCIPLE

The key to constantly making wise choices is by practicing what I call "Intelligent Mental Preparation" or simply IMP principle which means preparing yourself mentally to carefully and intelligently make those wise, satisfying and "un-regrettable" choices. The key here is that the moment you reach a point where you have to make that choice, especially those life threatening or the life changing ones, ask yourself the following questions:

- How is this choice going to affect me in both the short and long term?

- Is there a chance for me to regret making this choice tomorrow?

- How is this choice going to affect the people around me and my environment in general?

- Is this choice really worth making?

- What other options do I have?

Once you make a choice, take responsibility, accept and make peace with the choice you made and move on.

We live now in a very "hectic and fast paced life where everyone seems to be in a rush for different reasons. There is usually more than one option to choose from, and you cannot afford to always make quick and mentally unprepared choices which will lead you to losing your inner peace and become unhappy. Perhaps you might feel that sometimes you find yourself having only one option to choose from which can be debatable. The important lesson here is that, always try your best to slow down, clear your mind, if you have enough time, do your own research and get all the facts before making any decision. The idea is to make a wise choice that will eventually give you inner peace, joy and satisfaction.

Remember that we are where we are today because of the choices we made in the past, and therefore the choices we make today will surely determine our future and lead us into either regret or victory. Our past experiences and choices are equally important, whether negative or positive they provide great lessons to take into the future, and also to identify the errors we should not repeat. Note that the level of knowledge we have on a particular subject affects the choices we make which in return affects our decision making. This is the reason why it is so important to do our own research if we are about to make a choice. It starts with the little things such as the food we eat, spending or saving our money, reading a book or watching television, spending our major time on minor issues or using our time wisely and so on.

It is very important to learn and understand that everything affects everything else. We tend to ignore those small choices we make today forgetting that they will create a certain habit, which will eventually affect our future results. If we fail to make that little saving today, we will eventually have an empty bank account, if we fail today to love our children, our families and our friends, we will probably lose them later and wish we could have done things differently.

POISONOUS PEOPLE

I remember when I was still growing up and still in school at Itsose Primary School doing Standard Four. I had lots of misleading friends then and would often find myself in trouble for different reasons. I remember getting caught for unlawfully taking vehicle tires which were used for decoration at Miami-park near Dlomo Dam in Sharpeville. We wanted to burn them so we can get warm as it was still in winter and we would hang around at night enjoying our boy's chats and of cause share ideas on how to "catch" that one beautiful girl in the area.

We were about six and it was very dark, suddenly everyone started running. Unfortunately, I was the only one who got caught. I was beaten pretty badly by the police officer who had rings on eight of his fingers and with his fists, he was hitting me very hard on my face. I was later released after my father came to my rescue. I still remember the marks I had on my face even today, and I had to go to school the following day, you can imagine the embarrassment, not to mention the questions I had to answer.

I must say that I learnt my lesson from that experience. I made a personal decision that I will never again perform any unlawful activities and will be very careful when choosing friends. As I grew up over the years, I realized that we are all often surrounded by what I call poisonous people. Negative people who consciously or unconsciously influence our lives, the choices we make and also the decisions we take.

Sometimes we get into troubles due to negative ideas we get from our loved ones or perhaps our friends. Some people spend their precious time looking for mistakes and fault in others. When they are looking outside through the window on a shiny day, they only see and notice the specks on the glass and not the sun. I am sure you can already think of someone you know who always see faults in every little thing you do. People who always complain and blame everyone and everything without suggesting a better way or providing any solutions, these my friend are the poisonous people.

Sad but true, you will somehow have to make a tough choice and get rid of anyone you identify as toxic and poisonous if you really want to find inner peace and happiness in your life. This could be a challenging exercise to do since these people are mostly people very close to you. The few detoxing processes I know are not enjoyable at all, perhaps the better way which is usually recommended by the "health gurus" are methods of using herbs. The same applies when you go through a process of "detoxing" from people." Remember that you become the average of your five friends or close people you spend most your time with. Poisonous people are capable of affecting your skills and knowledge, your income, your health, your relationships, your career, your personal development and so on. As Jim Rohn says: "life does not get better by chance, it gets better by change". Here is one of my favourite quotes by Tamalee Sawyer on Pinterest which says: "The person you will be in five years is decided by the people you spend time with and the books you read today."

POISONOUS PEOPLE ELIMINATION PROCESS (PPEP)

If you surround yourself with poisonous people, your chances of finding inner peace are very limited. Poisonous people will always make sure you are on the path to darkness. You will likely keep on getting the same negative results over and over again until you start with what I call the "Poisonous People Elimination" (PPE) process. You run alongside losers, and you'll end up a loser, consciously or unconsciously. I grew up hearing a lot of the phrase "Birds of a feather flock together" and now I fully understand its meaning. Opinions of others don't really matter if they are not stopping you from achieving your major and minor goals. Someone's opinion of you does not define your reality. The key lesson here is that you should align yourself with positive, successful and motivated people with the same vision and goals as yours. These are the people who will help you with growth and empowerment. They will provide you with more skills, increase your knowledge and will surely keep on stretching you to grow even further as you will be learning from their daily activities, patterns and life philosophies. These are people who support you no matter what.

Here is the step by step process that I use on how to eliminate poisonous people:

- On a piece of paper preferably your journal, write down your purpose in life and your vision as clear as possible, this is your core reference for all you want to achieve.

- Make a list of all the people you spent most of your time with, friends, relatives, colleagues and so on.

- Setup a meeting with your immediate family and discuss your plans and goals, let them be aware of your purpose and vision, you need them for a support.

- On the list you made, identify all the people who add value to your plans, those having more or less the same vision as yours, if they are not in your list, then go out there and look for them. This could be a challenge, but you need people who already achieved what you are trying to achieve.

From the list identify all people who do not add value and are your time wasters, your main idea is to spend as minimal time with them as possible. Please remember that you do not really have to tell them about your plan, if they are "poisoning" you, then you need to remove the poison completely.

From the list, simply tick all those you are going to eliminate, those who you identified as poisonous.

Your focus must be on what you want to achieve, your end results and not to focus on the process for the process of achieving greatness is usually not pleasant, however do your best to enjoy the process. It is vitally important to know precisely: who you are, where you are going and most importantly what you really want?

Your answers to these three basic questions will make it easy for you to know what kind of people to attract in your life and who to choose as your true friends. If you want to keep getting what you are getting, then simply keep doing what you are doing and have been doing and keep these toxic people in your life. The opposite is also true, the key is, for things to start changing in your life, you must first change. Sometimes the person who needs you the most is the one you are looking at in the mirror.

I have learnt the hard way that when something bad happens to you, eighty percent of the people in our lives won't really care much and about fifteen percent will be glad that it is happening to you and just maybe the other five percent may give you support and encourage you to stand up again and go on. Have you ever noticed lately that when a person gets into physical trouble, say knocked by a car, or is drowning in a swimming pool, instead of trying to help the person, most people would rather take their cell phones and take pictures or videos?

If there is no enemy within, the outside one cannot harm us. Everything depends on you; you are the major key to your better future. The lesson is that make a wise choice and choose only the best people in your life. Choose those that keep stretching you and are always helping you to achieve your goals. The world on its own is a beautiful and safe place to be, only poisonous people make it look dangerous and harmful. One of the major principles to finding inner peace is by choosing to surround yourself with those with same vision, ideas and values as yours. People who have already achieved the same dreams you want to achieve.

And lastly, do remember that most of the poisonous people are at the bottom, which is already over-crowded. The good news is that the people you are looking for are at the top and there is still massive space available at the top. One of many reasons why the minority get very successful, find joy and inner-peace, is that if they find themselves in a path that is already over-crowded, they become bold enough to take a different path. It is very difficult to see where you are going if you are in an over-crowded path; for if the crowd falls, you too will fall. The only thing you need to do now is make a choice to take a different path; the path to light; simply by moving up just a bit and move up again until you reach the top. There is certainly power in making wise choices. As John C. Maxwell says: *"Life is a matter of choices, and every choice you make makes you"*.

Chapter 6: The Power of Choices

_____

_____

_____

_____

_____

_____

_____

_____

_____

_____

_____

_____

_____

_____

_____

_____

_____

_____

_____

_____

_____

_____

_____

Some Key Points To Remember

The choices you make today will determine your future success or failure.

The war is on between light and darkness, love and hate, internal conflicts and inner peace.

Prepare yourself mentally to carefully and intelligently make wise choices.

Your level of knowledge affect the choices you make.

Do your own research so you can make better and effective decisions.

The people you surround yourself with contribute to your success or failure.

Poisonous people are capable of influencing your joy and can steal your inner peace.

Start the process of Poisonous People Elimination (PPE). Someone's opinion of you does not define who you are.

You run along losers you simply end up a loser, choose your friends wisely.

My Personal Notes

_____

_____

_____

_____

_____

_____

_____

_____

"

"The choices we make today and
the ones we made in the past, will
determine our failure or success,
the key is to always do your best
and choose wisely."

Pheello Ntuka

PART 3

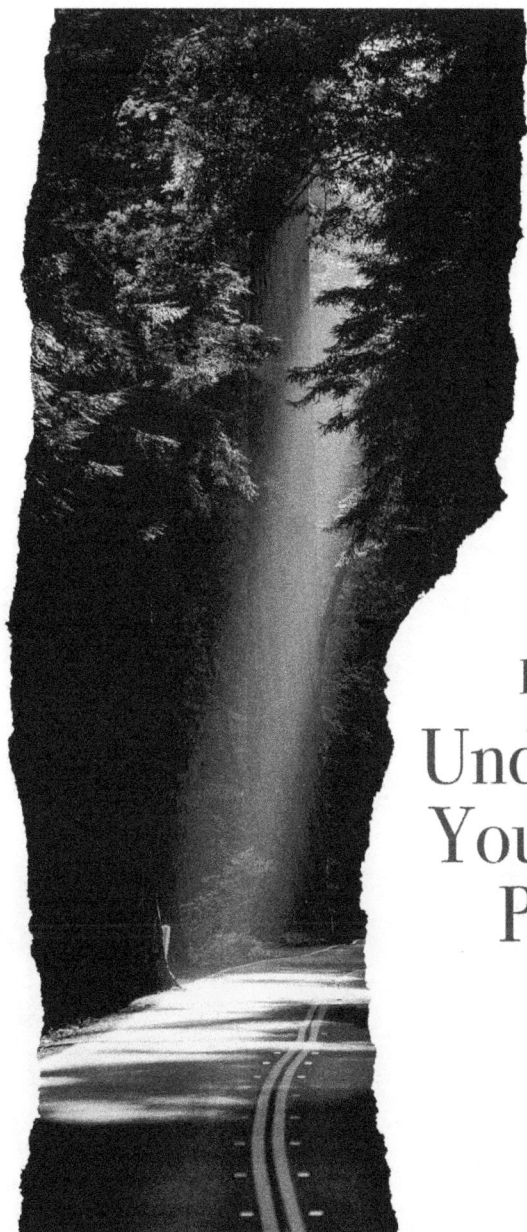

Understand Your Inner Power

CHAPTER 7

Emotions are a Powerful Driving Force

_____

In 2009 my wife and I went through yet another highly intense emotional experience. When we got the good news from the doctor that we were going to have our third child, we all got very excited. We could not wait to meet this precious gift from God. What we did not know was that, this excitement was going to be short lived. On our second visit to see our gynecologist, the doctor went through the normal process of checking weight and asking the questions that he usually asks. The moment came when he had to scan my wife's tummy checking how the baby was doing. We got a shock of our lives when he told us that he was not detecting our baby's heartbeat and immediately sent us to the nearest hospital for confirmation.

I am sure you understand clearly what that meant. It simply meant there was no new life anymore inside my wife's tummy but a lifeless fetus. We later got the confirmation from another scan and she had to go through an operation to get the fetus removed. We both started questioning God why that had to happen. Just like any person who loses their loved one through death, we felt lots of intense negative emotions. I am sure most parents can relate to this kind of sad experiences we sometimes have to go through. In my own opinion, there is no emotional pain similar to that of losing someone you love dearly through death.

As I write this chapter my wife has had to be admitted yet again to the hospital for gall stones and pancreas related illness. She had to face yet another operation to get the gall stones removed. I could easily tell from my daughter's faces that this was greatly affecting them emotionally. In my opinion a hospital theatre is one of the scariest places, for there is always fear of not coming back alive linked to this room.

In case you ask yourself, what does all this have to do with finding inner-peace, again I can assure you that it has a lot to do with it. Human beings are emotional creatures, we are all affected by how we feel, good or bad. You cannot find inner peace when you are experiencing negative emotions such as sadness, fear, guilt, shame, hatred, grief, anxiety, regret, blame, embarrassment and the list is endless.

There is a book that I recommend which explains more about emotions in more details by Gill Hasson: "Understanding

Emotional Intelligence: Pearson, 2014". There are other similar books of course in case you want to study the subject of emotions at the highest level.

My simple meaning of the word emotion is, a strong feeling produced by moods or circumstances. Emotions connect thoughts, feelings and actions. I have learnt late in my life the power of emotions, for they are the driving force of our lives. I cannot over emphasize the importance of constantly being aware of how you feel every moment of your life, for this will determine your actions and therefore your end results. When you are aware of how you feel about any situation or circumstance that you may be facing, you can easily choose a better option on how to deal with the situation and make a better decision.

We all react differently to various situations, depending on how we control our emotions and view that particular situation. How we read and give meaning to a specific event or situation will eventually determine our decision, our action and finally the end results. We may handle similar situations differently based on how we feel at the time of the event and the significance we place on it. When my wife was still in hospital preparing to undergo surgery, a representative of the account department at the hospital came to tell us that there was a co-payment of about R8000 we needed to pay before the operation could be performed.

We were told that we had to sign and commit ourselves to paying that amount or else she would have to be transferred to another hospital. Our medical aid had changed their policy with regards to admission fees and we were not made aware of this new policy amendment. My wife got very furious about the situation and almost lost her temper which is understandable. I on the other hand was calm, trying to get more clarity and find better ways to deal with the situation. This is just an example on how we react differently to similar situations. There is usually more than one option we can choose from when dealing with controlling our emotions. The meaning we give to our daily situations could either be positive or negative. We can all relate to situations where something happens to you and you somehow decide to associate it with some kind of bad luck. Perhaps you view the situation as a sign that your ancestors have abandoned you. Someone may view the same situation as a good sign that prosperity is knocking on the door. You can decide to give a positive meaning to the same situation with the view that change is necessary in order to start focusing on your high priority values.

EMOTIONS AND ITS MEANING

The meaning you give to any situation could lead to pain or pleasure. The key to always be positive about all the situations you come across and will lead to pleasurable results. The other side of the coin is also true, if you are negative about your daily situations you will simply feel emotions of sadness. I have learnt in my recent life experiences that every emotion is accompanied by a message. The message is linked to the significance you give to the situation. The sad part is that if you are negative when viewing the situation and cannot alter it, you will probably feel pain until you change your perception; and then the message will change. If for example you are nervous before that interview or have emotions of fear due to the unknown. Instead of associating these feeling with demons or some imagined monster. How about linking the situation with the message of being more prepared or becoming more aware and focused on what is more important. Due to our past beliefs and mental programs, we give negative messages to our daily situations by default. This usually happens in matter of milliseconds.

Every time I face an external negative situation or disturbing event, be it a phone call or an email, sad news, a scene on TV etc. First, I pause and ponder the situation by applying my mind and filtering out any negative interpretation. I then make myself aware of how I feel; if I feel bad or sad, I would question my thinking and look for better options to change how I feel. I then decide to act better and get pleasing result. There is usually feedback I get as

to whether I should act more, act less, change something or give up and move on. The whole idea is you want to contain your inner peace. The part of applying your mind is usually what is missing in this puzzle and often leads to bad decision making, undesired action and therefore unpleasing results. Here is my favorite key phrase: *"Master your psychology, master your emotions and get extraordinary joy and inner peace."*

Emotions are not triggered by what other say or do to us, but by the misconception that we do not have control over them. I have learnt that we are emotional creatures and we are fully capable of changing how we feel. The longer we stay on any negative state of emotion, the longer it will take us to find inner peace and therefore the results we want. Emotions are nothing but action signals carrying a message to either change how you perceive the situation or change your current procedure which could be not working so well. Emotions won't go away if you decide to suppress them, in most cases their intensity increases causing you more pain and increased stress.

Emotions always carry great messages and lessons, the more painful the event, the more profound the lesson. The things that usually break our hearts, are the very same things that actually serve to open them. Wisdom usually comes the hard way. The sooner you deal with your negative emotions; the sooner you will find inner peace. You actually force your mind to be in harmony with how you feel. This has to happen so you can end the internal war between your mind and your emotions. There is nothing good or bad about emotions, but the thinking makes it so. The meaning we attach or detach to the event or situation makes it either good or bad, positive or negative, encouraging or discouraging, loving or hating and so on.

YOUR EMOTIONAL AWARENESS

By being in control of your emotions, you become in control of every event or situation you come across and therefore your actions and finally your results. The alternate, if you lose control of your emotions, you also lose your power to be in control of handling the event or situation. One of my favorite phrases about emotions by Anthony Robbins is that, "Emotions create motion." If you create better emotions, you will surely create better motion or action, it is therefore very important to be the master of your inner-world. We all create our emotions consciously or unconsciously and this process is not automatic. The secret is to be fully aware of how you feel and understand that your emotions are not created by the environment or your surroundings. It is what we think about the environment or the event that occurred that created the emotion. This is something you can control and change at any moment, even when the external event is against you. How you perceive and interpret the event will determine your emotional mastery. Failure to regulate your day to day emotional difficulties such as fear, anxiety, anger, jealousy and incompetence will surely steal your joy and inner peace. Emotional awareness is what will give you the power to overcome any struggle and that temporary state of stagnation. When you are facing a negative emotion, pause a little bit before taking a conscious decision and try to measure the intensity of your emotion. A scale of 1 to 10 works marvelous, 1 being lowest intensity and 10 being the highest intensity.

Most of the events are average or of less intensity and therefore easy to deal with. However, if you measure an emotion to be on a scale of high intensity, anything from 6 to 10, this is the point where you have to apply what I call "Emotional stop and start process." This means stop a bit, ponder the event and start the event analyzing process, by looking at all positive, better and encouraging options so that you can be proud of your end result. Every decision you make has got its consequences; it is therefore necessary to first think about the consequences your emotion could cause before taking any action. Our prisons are full of people who lost control of their emotions and they ended up committing crime.

Negative feelings block you from succeeding and getting the results you want. It is not the circumstances in your life that determine your future, but how you deal with how you feel and the power you have over your emotions. Your interpretation of the event is key here. I have in my life heard people saying these words every time something happens: "If this happens, it means that…" I am sure you can relate; be very careful the moment you use this phrase. The meaning you give to any event is your actual interpretation. It is therefore important to be fully aware of your interpretations, negative interpretation will certainly provide negative action and therefore negative results. Why not give all your circumstance and events more positive empowering interpretations? This will surely require some practice, but it is something we can all learn. My life changed drastically after learning and practicing this major principle.

MASTER KEY TO INNER PEACE

Mastering your thoughts lead to mastering your emotions. When you master your emotions, you gain the power to control your reaction to every situation and circumstances in your life, and when all this happens, I can assure you that you will always find inner peace.

Thoughts create emotions, why do you feel happy or sad? If you get promoted to a higher level in your field of work, the promotion itself has actually no meaning and no value attached to it, you are the one assigning the meaning by your thinking, which you have absolute control over.

For most people, these thoughts are unconscious and have automatic meaning. When someone gets promoted, the first thing that comes to the mind is, promotion means more money which instantly mean happiness. If you are involved in an abusive or unpleasant relationship and you lose your partner due to break up or even divorce, you will surely feel a lot of negative emotions. If you decide to assign a false interpretation to your situation, you will soon or later feel sad or depressed. These negative emotions could eventually become highly intense. It is possible you will think the thoughts related to betrayal, loneliness, shame, miserableness, embarrassment or even suicide. It is vitally important to always monitor your thoughts for they affect your emotions. Emotions play a massive role in finding joy and inner peace. It is not possible to find peace if you are overwhelmed by negative emotions.

My belief is that we are all capable of controlling how we interpret all the situations we face. God is kind enough to have given a man a world class resource called the mind.

John Earl Shoaff's quote that has helped me sharpen my thinking says: "Don't wish it was easy, but wish you were better; don't wish for less problems but wish for more skills and lastly; don't wish for fewer challenges but wish for more wisdom." The sooner we learn and understand that problems and challenges are part of our lives, the sooner we are going to acquire the necessary skills to positively deal with them.

Emotions are simply signals that awaken us, they trigger us to pay attention to what is significant in our lives. Their function is mainly to prepare us for the worst that could happen so we can plan better. The big question is what kind of interpretations are you going to decide on, positive or negative?

Negative emotions will steal your peace, and if not dealt with positively, they will just keep on generating more negative feelings. You always have more than one option you can choose from in your internal world, therefore choose the interpretation that will give you peace. If you find yourself feeling sad or perhaps in a bad mood, quickly think about the things you are proud and grateful for and you will instantly feel happy and regain your peace. It is not possible to be sad and grateful simultaneously. Lazy negative interpretation leads to suffering. You will have less worries if you learn how to positively interpret circumstances and events to your own benefit and advantage.

Take full responsibility on all your negative emotions, don't blame external circumstances and point a finger to other people. The day I realized that no one is actually causing me to feel in any way, and accepted full responsibility on how I feel, I gained full control over my emotions and finally found my inner peace. Sometimes from the bitter experience, comes the greatest awakening. The same wall that keeps out disappointment also keeps our happiness, joy and peace.

"Let life touch you but not kill you, nothing can resist a human willpower, shortly put, do it or die" - *Jim Rohn.*

Some Key Points To Remember

Emotions are the powerful driving force capable of building or destroying.

Human beings are emotional creatures.

Learn and practice how to control your emotions.

See your emotions as signals carrying specific messages to act upon and give them positive empowering meanings.

Always be aware of how and what you feel.

Your inner peace relies on your thinking and how you feel.

Decide to positively interpret your unforeseen circumstances by finding what is positive and empowering.

Accept that problems and challenges will remain part of our lives. There is always more than one option you can choose from in your internal war and inner conflicts.

Mastering your thoughts is the key to mastering your emotions.

My Personal Notes

_____

_____

_____

_____

_____

_____

_____

"

"Whenever you experience any
difficulty and emotional pain, make
it your commitment to maintain
your inner peace by searching
for positive meanings."

Pheello Ntuka

CHAPTER 8

Review Your Belief System

In this chapter I would like to touch on yet another basic principle that affects our joy and inner peace either negatively or positively. My definition and understanding of a belief is an idea that is supported by evidence, due to its repetition, it becomes a habit which eventually form a behavior.

We all behave and do things mainly due to how our belief system is shaped, consciously or unconsciously. When we grew up, there were lot of beliefs that were installed into our subconscious mind by our parents, surroundings and environment. You could be following someone's opinion which turned into a belief and has been used and followed by your previous generations. This belief might not necessarily be true or untrue. As a baby when you are born, you come to this world with absolutely no beliefs. The big question is how and when did we realize that we now suddenly believe in something so much that if affects us in all different areas of our lives?

In case you are asking yourself what I am talking about, let me explain, beliefs are formed in our brain from when we are as little as 3 years old. All the little things we observe and listen to from our parents, our community or in school form our beliefs.

I remember when I was still a little boy, my parent used to tell me that I should not cut my nails inside the house, a myth was that if you cut your nails in the house there will be fights and arguments. In school, most of us were made to believe that those who get higher marks will have a bright and successful future and those like myself who used get average marks would never be successful. It was even worse if you were consistently getting far below average marks. Words are very powerful, I remember some of us were being called words like "domkop (dumb-head), houtkop (wood-head), silly-fool, useless, "gemors" (rubbish), setlatla (stupid) and the list is endless. I am sure those who are my age can relate to this. The sad part of this is that that fact that we were called these words by our parents and some of our teachers, we saw ourselves as dumb and stupid. These words installed limiting beliefs in us which affected our self-esteem, our self-confidence, our self-courage, our intelligence and capabilities.

It is very important to be very careful who and what we listen to, for it can severely affect our belief system. Statements like "nobody likes you, you are useless and worthless, you have an ugly face, and your birth was unplanned" and so on, affect how we see ourselves. It also affects how we see the world and lowers our self-esteem which in return affects our inner-peace. Our beliefs shape our entire future, it is therefore very critical that we review our beliefs and refine them to be in line with our goals and dreams. This is one of many reasons why we fail to achieve our goals and getting our desired outcomes.

Our beliefs affect every little thing we do. If you are not happy about anything, change it, if your plan is not working well, change it. One of my favorite motivational phrase by Les Brown that helps me in achieving most of my goals is, *"If it is worth doing, then it is worth doing badly until you get it right."*

Reviewing and amending your belief system is another part of your life that is worth doing so it can benefit you and not work against you. I have learnt that courage is really not something that comes deep from inside, but it is when you are afraid and want to do something you believe is worth doing, then you do it anyway. It is amazing how we are affected by little things we are not even aware of. Everything affects everything, BUT, (note there is a big "but" here), "only few things matter." Things like where we were born or where we grew up, all install beliefs in our subconscious mind and develop our self-image. Self-image is simply how you see yourself.

WHAT ARE YOUR MOST DOMINANT BELIEFS?

The world today is mostly surrounded by negative information and uncertainties. If you spent most of your time watching television and listening to your local radio station. I am sure you will agree with me that almost over eighty percent of what is viewed and broadcasted is negative, from the news to some radio shows, short stories on television and some music videos etc.

Thanks to the power of internet, we now have a choice to watch what we presume to be important and beneficial to us. The main challenge is that our children believe so much in what they see and perceive as a good life from the television. The more you find yourself in negative surroundings and associations, the more limiting beliefs you install and process into your life. This is what affects our life philosophies, views, opinions, choices and perspectives. You are either living by someone else's plan and belief or your own, aware or unaware, so why not design you own plan and belief system?

We are constantly trying to figure ourselves out by juxtaposing ourselves to the most influential people in the country and in the world. One can for example compare the former first black President of the country and the most recent former President, depending on his or her views, opinions and decisions, a belief system is suddenly installed. Each one of us from childhood to adulthood have developed dominant beliefs, these beliefs makes it very hard for you to see things differently.

Be fully aware of your past installed beliefs and review them. If they are still giving you the results you are looking for, then that's fine, no need to change them. But if for some reason they limit you, maybe is the time to consider changing them towards your advantage. The core beliefs such as ego, identity, faith and emotions are the most dominant beliefs that affects us consciously or unconsciously. An event might have happened in your past and perhaps was not dealt in properly, this event could lead to self-hate, pride, fear, jealousy, anger, worthlessness and low self- esteem. All these limiting beliefs will certainly steal your inner peace if you don't make the necessary amendments by reviewing and refining your core beliefs.

Some beliefs were installed in us without our awareness and keep us hostage for many years. These leads to living by default, doing what the crowd does, thinking the same thoughts as your peers and associates. It can also have a major impact on how we feel about ourselves, our self-image and the world in general.

BELIEF CAN BE LINKED TO PLEASURE OR PAIN

I really would like to over-emphasize the importance of taking time to reflect and refine your belief system. This is one major part of our lives that contributes to finding peace within, whether we are aware of it or not. Your belief system affects your entire life. All your misinterpreted experiences can also create your belief system, for example if somewhere in your life you loved someone who rejected you, you then develop a belief that no one will ever love you. I am sure you can relate to this experience. Some of our beliefs can cause more pain than pleasure in our lives.

The way we see the world and ourselves is shaped by our beliefs. It is for this reason that if you really want to constantly have inner peace in your life, at least consider reviewing and refining your belief system. If you can find ways to link most of your experiences with more pleasure that pain, then why not opt for this choice, for it will certainly bring more peace and joy into your life.

BELIEFS FOR SURVIVAL

There are other types of beliefs we seem to ignore, and these are the beliefs for survival. I am sure you are probably wondering what this means. Let me explain. These beliefs also affected our great grandparents and were passed on to our generation and now we are unconsciously passing it on to our children who are as well probably going to do the same. As a young child, my father used to say if I can go to school, then my future will be bright, and I can have anything I want. I was made to believe that I will find all the answers I am looking for in school. I later in my life found out that this is half the truth.

From grade one to twelve is a full twelve-year period if you don't repeat a grade. My short memory of the things I have learnt in that twelve years consists of a mixture of value-added subjects such as languages, mathematics, agriculture just to mention a few. The other side were topics which fall under my list of "not much." Anything that does not make "much impact" towards my purpose and vision falls under this list. I still remember learning about frogs, lizards, fish, locusts just to name a few. Those who are my age can relate to this. I must confess that some of the subjects I was learning about in my school days did not really make a good impact and contribution when I reached my adult life and my work life.

There is also a positive side that I will forever be grateful for. The other fifty percent luckily secured me a job which helped to be what I am today and again I am grateful for it. During these years I managed to meet lot of really great people, from my former teachers, colleagues and lot of people I still interact with till today. Below are part of my beliefs and experiences in relation to formal education as compared to self-education. Please ponder these beliefs and make your own analysis and conclusion. We have to become good students and not followers, we look at both negatives and positives about formal education.

If you do well in formal education, you get to have a recognized qualification or a certificate related to what you have studied with your full name on, this is your key that allows you knock on those doors during your job hunting, or when you are looking for a promotion or you want to study further.

The problem comes when you fail, you are seen as a failure, this install a limiting belief full of self-doubt, low self-esteem and a belief of not being good enough.

Self-education taught me that failing is just a feedback on how not to do something and that failing is what leads to success. I installed a new belief that failing is actually good for it is what makes one to eventfully succeed.

Self-education also gives the power to learn more on specific things you are really interested in and which is of your highest value, there is freedom of choice here.

Most of the people work on jobs that are not aligned to what they were taught in school or universities. There is no doubt how much money one spent to have a good formal education qualification; the sad part is that there are no guarantees that one will find a good paying job. This in my own opinion is a plan of disaster.

The majority of the people fight hard to at least get good matric results so they can be admitted in universities with the hope to eventually find a good paying job. I am not saying the formal education is bad, but I believe it is only half the equation. I still wonder who decides on the curriculum, its mission and objectives, this could be a good debate for another day.

The moment you face the reality of life you will probably understand what I am taking about. Life in your workplace and life after retirement are two different types of best experiences, we can all learn from. I have seen people struggling while they are still working and even worse after their retirement. Those who run successful businesses will agree with me that they had to start everything from the beginning, learning how to start and run their businesses. My belief is that formal education gets you a job, but self-education is what makes you thrive. Financial education teaches us that a job gives you wages or salary, but a business is what gives you fortune.

Note that a belief could be both true and untrue, depending on how you look at it. We could both be looking at half-glass of water, you might see it as half-empty and I could see it as half-full. It is therefore very important to choose our beliefs wisely for they affect and determine our current and future results.

Here is one of my favourite philosophies: *"your results affect your joy and inner peace, fruitful results give you joy and inner peace, but unfruitful ones gives you sadness."*

We accept certain beliefs not by our own choices but because of survival requirements. Beliefs are made up and then were given specific meaning, these meanings are not necessarily true. Some of our sisters find themselves believing that the easy way to make money is by selling themselves and becoming the slaves to those who wants to satisfy their external need such as lust. They then develop a belief that they are worthless and have no value in the society. Poverty also made most of our brothers and sisters to believe that God does not exist for they go to church with the hope of improving their lives, guess what happens to their self-esteem if they don't find this. Churches are being run as businesses and playgrounds lately. These are the beliefs for survival that I am talking about. Everyone has a certain belief about all topics and issues related to life. Review and refine your beliefs system to your advantage so you can live a peaceful life.

HOW TO REFINE AND CHANGE YOUR BELIEFS

Why not work on a plan to rise above all the limiting beliefs that affect you daily? Some of the ideas from our parents, other major influencers such as the community, members of your church, your colleagues, your close friends and relatives could have a major impact on your belief system.

The little voice in your ears that keep on screaming and telling you that you are not good enough, you are worthless, you are ugly and have no value comes from your beliefs. God created each and every one of us to serve a specific purpose. He gave us the potential and all the resources to change the world, serve His purpose and fight against the devil's work. Your belief system could make your world look like this ugly monster that is very hard and full of struggle and suffering. We all have past stories that make us believe that life is dangerous and tough. This makes us afraid of the unknown, so what's your story? Even those people who we regarded as smartest, perhaps passed with seven distinctions, also have limiting beliefs.

The three main limiting beliefs are hopelessness, helplessness and worthlessness.

Hopelessness says: it won't happen for me and no use to even try, it is only for the rich people or it is only for those who are educated and have high level of skills.

Helplessness says: I don't have the abilities to do it, I do not have the resources, I am too weak, I am too afraid, and people will laugh at me.

Worthlessness says: I don't deserve it, I am not good enough, they won't like me, I have no value, I am not important.

We are most chained and jailed because of one if not all of these core limiting beliefs. It is very important to recognize them so we can develop a plan to break them and free ourselves from the limitations they bring.

Here is the truth, the belief "I am not ...." is a lie. Before it was agreed upon, it was someone else's opinion, this opinion was a fallacy. You can argue with someone and influence their belief system. Some will still not hear your facts because of their strong high level of belief, negative or positive, and this is called belief confirmation. We have seen many times when an alcoholic or a smoker trying to quit these habits and after some time, they return to their core beliefs. Due to uncertainty and high level of stress, they go back to their existing belief system. The longer you hold on to the belief, the more it creates roots that goes deeper into your subconscious mind.

We were all born with no beliefs; therefore, beliefs are like skills, and they were all learnt and can thus be unlearned. There is a phrase that I like which says, "Those that achieve massive success are those who can learn, unlearn and relearn." The good news is that you can reshape and unlock your beliefs. There is a strong link between the mind, emotions and the body. What you think and believe will affect how you behave and perform. It is a must to shape your life in such a way that it will benefit you and not work against you. How you behave, the choices you make, your performance and the outcomes are shaped entirely by your belief system. Your beliefs are affecting your joy and inner peace.

Here are the few steps that helped me to change my belief system. Identify your belief toward your specified goal, ask yourself what is it that you must believe in to achieve this goal, compare that with your current belief. For example, if you want a good happy marriage, what are your current beliefs with regards to marriage and what beliefs do you think will help you become a happy spouse. Decide and say no more to your previous belief, you don't have to tell anyone when you change your belief. Simply say to yourself, I used to believe in this, now I believe in something new, for example: I used to believe that I am worthless and now I believe I am worthy or I used to believe that I am not good enough, now I believe in my abilities.

Engage new positive information, surround yourself with valuable, prosperous, encouraging information.

Associate yourself with people who will have a positive impact on your future belief system.

Surround yourself with quality people - positively minded ambitious and highly productive people are the ones you look for.

Act and move forward, work consistently on your new beliefs so they become part of you.

Inside of each and every one of us, is a greater version of ourselves, sometimes it takes just one person to tell you that you are special, beautiful, loved, capable and worthy. I am hoping that this chapter will make you realize this and the power you have over all these limiting beliefs so you can start accumulating more joy and inner peace in your life.

When I was still studying in tertiary, I did not believe in myself at all, self-doubt was part of me, today I am very proud of myself, my success and my achievements. You are a wonderful being created by God to serve a special purpose, and not just to add numbers. It is therefore important to embrace empowering beliefs. As Wayne Dyer says: " *A belief system is nothing more than thought you've thought over and over again*".

Some Key Points To Remember

Review your belief system and make the necessary changes.

Our past knowledge and experiences make up and form our current belief system.

Be very careful what and who you listen to and follow as your leader. Search, review and keep on refining your most dominant beliefs.

Your life philosophy is affected by current belief system.

Most beliefs were installed or programmed into your mind without your awareness.

Beliefs can be linked to pleasure or pain.

A belief can be true or untrue depending on how you perceive it to be.

Intelligence has got nothing to do with beliefs. You become what you believe so much in.

My Personal Notes

_____

_____

_____

_____

_____

_____

_____

_____

66

"The time is now to change your belief system, simply by believing in yourself, therefore review, refine and change your belief system to benefit you so you can find joy and inner peace."

Pheello Ntuka

CHAPTER 9

Improve Self-Discipline

———————————

One of the major differences between successful and not so successful people is the ability to apply self-discipline in every situation. My simple definition of self-discipline is the ability to do what must be done whether you feel like it or not.

It is a constant awareness of the need for action and a conscious act to implement that action. There is a direct relationship between self-discipline and procrastination. Procrastination says, "I might do it tomorrow instead of doing it today, and I may do what I can and not what must be done." Discipline on the other hand says, "Do it now and do it to the best of your ability whether you feel like it or not." There is a book which I highly recommend by Brian Tracy: "Eat That Frog: Berrett-Koehler Publishers Inc, 2007" which explains procrastination in more detail.

You can do everything right, have a master plan and become as highly motivated as you possibly can, but if you lack self-discipline, you lower your chances of attaining your goals. Self-discipline is a never-ending process, it is ongoing. The minute you set a goal, whether small or big, your goal achievement is largely dependent on how you are going to discipline yourself. Disciplining yourself to execute and act is the key to your success.

Achieving any goal simply by practicing self-discipline on a daily basis is a great motivator. When it (self-discipline) is high, procrastination has got no hold over you. In my world of technology, self-discipline is like the central processing unit (CPU) of any device, nothing functions well without the CPU in action. It is the core of any activity, for it leads to the outcome.

Think of a soccer team with little to no discipline. A coach might come up with the best tactical plan in the world. If the whole team lacks the discipline to stick to the coach's instruction, what do you think will happen to that team? The defenders will probably fail to defend well enough and the midfielders will also fail to distribute those passes and therefore the strikers will surely fail to score goals. This could mean that the team will lose the match by a large margin.

Knowledge is the potential key to success, but consistently disciplining yourself to applying that knowledge is the master key to success. Delay in personal success is mainly caused by lack of discipline.

I have learnt that self-discipline is actually not easy to master and practice. It requires a high level of determination and enough reasons why you want to achieve your goals. Your big "Why" is key here, for it is the driving force of self-discipline.

If for some reason you have five goals that you want to achieve in a certain time frame. It is very critical that you prioritize them and link them to specific reasons. The first goal given a high priority and linked to its why will be the one you focus on. Remember energy flows where focus is, and it then becomes easy to constantly discipline yourself to do whatever it takes to accomplish this one specific goal. One of the secrets I have learnt not long ago is that, highly successful people focus on one particular task at the time, they might look like they are doing lot of things all at the same time, but most of them use the power of delegation.

They delegate some other tasks to others they are working with. This gives them more time to probably start preparing for a new task or project. The major key here is that you must have enough reasons why you want to achieve your goals.

The following questions are important to be responded to: What value is achieving this goal going to add to your life?

How is not achieving this goal going to affect you in terms of your happiness, feelings, psychologically and your surroundings? Be clear on this for it serves as your driving force to disciplining yourself as you encounter challenges, you will be lying to yourself if you think everything will go smooth, "Clarity is power."

LITTLE THINGS COUNTS MORE

I have a helper who is like a brother to me. He told me a sad story about someone he knows very well. This person got involved in a car accident and was hospitalized for over six months. Unfortunately, he later died after he was discharged from the hospital. The accident was the result of him to ignoring the little things. He said this person's front car tyres were worn out to a point that you could literally see the small wires on those tyres. His reasoning was that he is trying to save money by not buying new ones.

Taking a life-threatening risk with the view of saving money in my own opinion is a bad idea. A tyre might cost you plus or minus a thousand rand depending on the size, but life is priceless. You lose it once; it is gone forever. The truth is that the absence of self-discipline can easily send a person to the graveyard. We have our brothers and sisters who lost their relationships and marriages through cheating. They lacked self-discipline and allowed lust to take control of their mind and emotions. When all this happens, your joy and inner peace will also be affected.

Increasing and improving your level of self-control on a daily basis is the key to having a high level of self-discipline. Self-control according to my understanding is an immediate short-term process, controlling yourself on those little daily activities, defeating those daily temptations. If for example you set a goal to lose a few kilograms and you find yourself shopping or in a mall at the food-court, it is very easy to end up buying the type of food which goes against your planned diet. Self-control is the ability to control yourself in that moment.

By consistently applying self-control in your daily life, you are in turn increasing your level of self-discipline. Failure to control yourself on those little daily activities will eventually lead to disaster and misery, which will in turn lower your self-esteem and self-confidence. I am sure we can all relate to having a day well planned and suddenly you realize that it is time for bed, and you did not do a quarter of those important tasks you wanted to do. That is bound to make anyone feel a little down and joyless.

An important fact to remember here is that, repetition of these little errors will create a habit of lack of self-control and eventually lack of self-discipline. Of cause the inverse of this is also true. By consistently doing the little things you planned for the day, you will in turn create a repetition of little successes which will form great habits, this will automatically increase your level of self- esteem and self-confidence. This in the process will also lead you into becoming a high goal achiever. The good news is that both self-control and self-discipline are learnable behaviors.

FAILURE VS SUCCESS

Delay in personal success in mainly caused by lack of self-discipline. Daily we learn how to do things by gathering knowledge, but we still fail to meet our objectives. Why do we still fail if we have all the knowledge and skills in the world? The answer lies in the absence of self-discipline.

Disciplining ourselves to apply all that we know is the master key here. Knowledge is only the potential to success, but the application of knowledge is what eventually leads to success. It does not matter how much you know or how smart you may be if you are not going to use it. It takes self-discipline to defeat that negative voice in our minds that tells us we cannot achieve great things.

- Failure to do the little things such as:
- Waking up on time.
- Arriving on time at your workplace.
- Not drinking enough water daily.
- Not walking to keep fit.
- Not spending time with family.
- Not saving or investing a percentage of your income.
- Not reading a book.
- Not attending developmental seminars or workshops
- Not attending church and connect with God and other believers.

These are just some of few little things that can easily become habits that soon lead to unwanted destinations. Lack of discipline leads towards a path to darkness which guarantees a joyless life with no inner peace. Your self-discipline determines your level of success. It takes great self-discipline to admit your mistakes and be totally honest with yourself by not allowing ego to take over. It takes serious discipline to be firm and respond in a calm professional way when negative opinions are thrown at your face.

DISCIPLINE IN TIME AND PRIORITY MANAGEMENT

I have learnt that success in every aspect of our lives is dependent of another major principle which is your ability to manage your time and priorities effectively. In my own life experience, I have realized that it is difficult to manage time but a lot easier to manage your priorities.

Whenever I set a specific major goal and break it down into small phases, the only way I know of to make the goal a success, is by defining these phases in terms of priorities. If you try to do lot of tasks simultaneously, the result is usually chasing your own tail. All great leaders have their quality of self-discipline in common, the key to executing and achieving any goal is therefore great self-discipline.

Self-discipline is the root of success and it is what attracts people to you. I have discovered that people like and admire those with a consistent high level of self-discipline. When you manage your

priorities well, this means you will by default practice what you preach and this in turn will make you a trustworthy person, people will trust you simply because you are a person of your word.

Have you ever found yourself having to attend two events on the same day and perhaps at the same time? Say for instance you get two invitations from two people that are both important to you, what do you do? And you really don't want to disappoint any of them. This is where your priorities come to your rescue for it should be easy to pick an event that is in line with your purpose or vision. If you have a clear vision and purpose that you need to serve, this will actually help you to know where your priorities lie. The secret here is that if you have a clear life purpose, your life priorities also become clear. Your life becomes very narrow in the sense that you can easily eliminate anything that is not aligned with your purpose. This principle on its own will certainly simplify your life as well as your choices. The minute you know where you are going, by default you will know which roads will take you there. You also know which path won't take you to your destination. Disciplining yourself to adhere and abide by your own life purpose and effectively managing your priorities is very significant. If someone offers you anything that is not aligned to your purpose, it becomes easy to refuse the offer and request it to be given to someone who might need that offer. Remember that no one was born to do everything, and the key phrase here is to learn that "Only few things are necessary" in our lives.

My life experiences have taught me that stress is usually generated by not knowing what to do. Incompetence also causes lot of stress and affects many people which in turn steals their joy and inner peace. It is even worse when you are not aware that you lack certain knowledge or skills, for this is like a death sentence, "not knowing that you don't know what you are supposed to know", and this could be due to either ignorance or lack of self-discipline. Discipline yourself to learn, you don't have to like certain things but at least learn them, what if you did not know that there is an acid which looks exactly like the water we drink or what if we did not know about the law of gravity you found yourself on top of a tenth building floor and you decide to jump?

A clear life purpose will choose your friends, your future, your priorities, the books you read, your daily "to do" list and plans, values and most importantly how you behave.

The major life lesson I have learnt is that we were all created by God to serve others and make a difference, and we can only achieve this by constantly improving our level of self-discipline. The only way I know how to measure your level of self-discipline is by using your own "Progress scale of achieved goals", this is now your daily set of goals, your weekly goals, monthly and yearly goals that you set for yourself. It is better to make a small progress than waiting for a perfect planned goal which might not be fulfilled. Learn to measure your progress daily. There more you achieve a certain number of goals the easier you can tell if you are progressing or not and therefore you can also tell and measure your level of self-discipline. "Self-discipline is the number one delineating factor between the rich, the middle class and the poor" - by Robert Kiyosaki.

"The number of goals you achieve is a measure of your progress, this also reveals your level of self-discipline."

-Pheello Ntuka

"Self-discipline is determined by the number of set goals achieved and their level of progress, low or high."

-Pheello Ntuka

_____
_____
_____
_____
_____
_____
_____
_____
_____
_____
_____
_____
_____
_____
_____
_____
_____
_____
_____
_____
_____
_____

Some Key Points To Remember

Always improve your self-discipline.

Procrastination says, "I might do it tomorrow." Discipline yourself to do and complete all the little tasks at hand.

Increase your level of self-control.

Delay in personal success is mostly caused by lack of discipline.

Talents and skills unused perish.

Discipline yourself to manage your priorities well.

Your achieved number of goals determine your level of self-discipline.

Be a person of your word.

People admire those with consistent high level of discipline.

My Personal Notes

_____

_____

_____

_____

_____

_____

_____

_____

_____

66

"Self-discipline is determined by the number of set goals achieved and their level of progress, low or high."

Pheello Ntuka

CHAPTER 10

Miracles of Massive Action

When I was still growing up in my primary school days, I used to see my father waking up at 04:00 every day going to work, whether it was very cold in winter or heavily raining in summer. No matter what was happening, he would still wake up early and go to work, sometimes on both Saturday and Sunday. What I did not understand then was that he had a mission to accomplish. His mission was that, as a father, he had to fulfil his purpose by making sure that he put food on the table and that my younger sister and I go to school, have a roof over our heads and so on. He had to make sure that he provides us with support and all the human basic needs. I would also observe other fathers who would just sit in the sun throughout the day and let their children starve. I also understood that this was probably due to not knowing what to do since they could not find jobs and they lived their lives based on hope. It was not difficult for me to compare those who were getting the results and those who were not. I also decided at a very young age that I did not want to work as hard as my farther did, and again I also didn't want to be like the other fathers who were depending on hope. I knew I had to learn and do things very differently. One thing that I am grateful for and will always be, is the fact that my father worked very hard just for us to go to school. Just like any other parent, his belief was that if he could provide us with education, we would be able to achieve absolutely anything. The reason I share this story is to highlight that your results and rewards will always depend on the actions you take.

Let us define action, my meaning of action is simply doing the work in order to achieve a specific goal, going to labour. In the last few years I have actually learnt that education is only 10 percent of the equation. In this chapter we will look into this in a broader view and consider all possible aspects of what I call the miracles of taking massive action.

All the principles that we covered in this book form part of the learning process which if studied properly, will lead to massive success, joy and inner peace. Knowledge is the potential power, but applied knowledge is what will give you power.

Here is the key process of learning that I believe all the successful people apply to their lives. First, they learn (information)

Second they practice (application),

Third they measure the results (experience)

Finally, they keep on refining their philosophy (wisdom).

Most of the people stuck in the first part, these days there is a lot of information available at our fingertips.

Too much information can lead to confusion and destruction. Have you ever met someone who seems to know every little thing? These people would give you advice on every topic even when you didn't ask for it. Most of them still struggle just to get their lives in order and are unable to take control of their own lives but, I tell you, they know it all.

Too much knowledge can frustrate you, especially when you preach what you don't practice, and your actions get confused by not knowing what you suppose to do. Here is what I have learnt and practiced which I believe is the reason I achieve my goals with ease. I have seen some of my friends, my colleagues and relatives with high qualifications still struggling to get their lives under control and achieving very little result. This is because they actually rest behind their high qualifications hoping their precious papers will do the work and the talking on their behalf.

The last two and half years I was blessed by being appointed a manager. This appointment somehow gave me the opportunity of being on the other side and becoming part of the panel in an interview and also to have people directly reporting to me. This is where I have realized that most people do not want to do the work, but they definitely want to get paid come pay day.

The most interesting part of this is that those who really hate coming to work, the laziest of them all, always complain about their salary not being enough and how they deserve better. I must admit that not all who are highly qualified behave this way. On the other side, those who are not so "highly qualified" as they say, are not complaining and are always willing to do more than expected. I guess the reason for this could be that they depend on their actions, efforts and abilities more that the qualifications. In my experience in the corporate world, these are the people who achieve more in their lives and excel in all they do. This brought me a conclusion that actions speak louder than words, no action means no results, less activity means low rewards, high action means high result and lastly extraordinary actions leads to extraordinary results and therefore extremely high rewards.

ACTION AND LAWS

One of the greatest lessons I have learnt in the past as a student and as an employee is that our lives are governed by laws, and laws if obeyed will lead to certain outcomes. This means laws are created for everyone to act and behave in a certain way. On the other hand, disobeying laws could lead to misfortune and ultimate failure.

Please note that there is a difference between laws and rules. Rules are usually created by one individual or a small group of people and usually for their own benefit, however, laws comes from the creator of a product so it can perform its original purpose and for the protections of the creator's reputation. If you break the rules, you can always get away with it.

Most successful people break the rules, but they make sure they obey the laws. If you disobey the laws of a specific thing, your actions will certainly not be aligned with the intended purpose of that thing and your chances of failing will be extremely high. This is the real reason I believe most people get stuck in what they are trying to achieve. Everything has got its basic laws for it to operate at its optimum level and these laws are the map of the actions to be taken. For example, if you buy a car, the manufacturer of that car will attach a manual with some basic laws. For instance, the car would need petrol to function and perform at its best, what if because you feel paraffin is less in price and decide to pour paraffin into the car's petrol tank? I am sure you can just imagine what would happen to the mechanics and performance of that car. This is what happens if we disobey the laws of the manufacturer and act the opposite to what the law requires us to do.

The critical part of this subject is that our lives also have laws that we must obey so we can live an effective successful life, life full of joy and inner peace. There are laws to everything, the difficult part is trying and learn all of them.

My view is that once you know and understand your purpose and the intention of your creator, half of your problems will be solved. This means you will only focus on the few laws to learn and your actions will also be manageable and aligned to that purpose, you won't be feeling overwhelmed at all.

Laws and our actions are related, this process affects even the little things we do in our day to day lives such as making a cup of tea or coffee, cleaning your pool, driving your car, managing your money, exercising, living a healthy lifestyle, raising a child, maintaining a good relationship with spouse and the list is endless. The following are just few examples of the laws that we live by and that must be obeyed, the actions we take on these laws will also guarantee success, joy, inner peace or ultimate failure.

- Government Laws, Tax and Public Laws

- Traditional and Cultural Laws

- Religious Laws or Biblical Laws

- Financial Laws

- Human Nature and Health Laws

- Marriage and relationship Laws

- Laws of the universe

- Corporate Laws

- Labour Laws

Laws are designed to protect, keep order and promote life. Laws guarantee peace, laws create norms. Obedience to laws guarantees success, joy and inner peace, therefore it is vitally important to always watch your actions.

I am certainly not a guru on matters of the law. The reason why I mention these laws here is that laws affect our actions and if disobeyed, the chances of living a joyful and peaceful life are very limited. We all know of someone who broke the law and found themselves in prison, simply because of the actions they chose to take.

Everything in life is designed to function by laws, this is the reason why success and failure are both predictable. Your action will always tell everything about you. If you spent too much time sitting on your comfortable couch watching television every day, this action is a sign of time wasting and therefore leads to failure. Again if you use your time effectively by planning your day in advance, setting those goals and working on them daily, applying the principle of learning a new thing in your field every day, practicing what you have learned, reviewing your progress and making those follow up then, by law, you are bound to succeed and find inner peace. In short, success is dependent of specific actions we do every day which are supposed to be aligned with the creator's laws. This includes but is not limited to, our intelligence, focus, courage, hard-work, our ideas, how we use our time, self-esteem and self- confidence, our mental strength and emotions, how we motivate ourselves and our willingness to do the work required in order to achieve massive success, joy and inner-peace.

DEVELOP THE ABILITY TO ACT TODAY, NOT TOMORROW

Life is 10 percent what happens, 90 percent is what you do and react to what has happened. What happens, happens to all of us, how you react to what has happened is what matters most. The best time to act, is when the idea is still hot, act when the emotion is still high and strong.

Jim Rohn says, *"Everything unused will perish, whatever you don't use, you lose."* Develop the ability to act when the energy is high, when the emotions are strong. Massive action taken today will always overpower procrastination, you cannot save today's energy for tomorrow. Today unused is lost forever. Talent and the ability unused are lost. Act today, not tomorrow.

If you want to build a library, you must first buy the first book, then the second and so on, sooner or later you will have many books, the important action to take is starting. The popular global organization "Nike" put it in another way "Just Do It"

The law of diminishing intent says, a good intention not done gets harder to do the longer it is delayed. If you do not convert your intentions into actions, soon the intent will start to diminish. If you wait for next month or next year, your idea and that powerful emotion will soon fade away and that will result in ultimate failure. Setup a discipline to act when the ideas and emotions are strong, high and powerful. If you are like me trying to get in shape, start today to do those push-ups, walking around the block, get that nutritional book today, not tomorrow. If you do not take immediate action then the wisdom is wasted, as they say, the greatest treasures and wisdoms of this world are found in the cemetery. Do not die with the music still playing in you and those talents still in you.

BABY STEPS PROCESS (SLOWLY BUT SURELY)

Here is what is important about action; all actions affect each other, and everything affects everything else. If you buy that one book, it will encourage you to read another book, if you eat a fruit a day and drink those required glasses of water daily, this will soon motivate you to take a walk and do those push-ups and sit-ups. You will soon be living a healthy lifestyle.

The opposite side of the coin is also true, if you ignore these important activities, soon you will be a regular at your local hospital. Some things are more important than others and that is a fact, but all other things do matter. Every let down affects your key performance and abilities. When you complete your first action and accomplish the little results you become inspired to take even more action. The key here is to reduce your lack of action and start the new process of developing yourself.

If you don't act, your psychology and consciousness gets affected and your own philosophy will be affected. Little unrecognized actions build up to a recognized final product. Today's action affects your tomorrow.

The good news is that if you get off track, you can always review your mistakes and get back on track. Most people are after instant gratification and have no patience to apply the baby steps process, slowly but surely. Sometimes you will have to choose between short-term pain or the long-term pleasure, the pain of discipline or the pain of regret.

ACTION IS THE MOTHER OF SUCCESS, JOY AND INNER PEACE

Most people learn stuff but never apply a bit of what they have learned. You could be a sincere, dedicated, loving and caring person who attends classes, workshops and reading books, but for as long as you don't apply this knowledge, finding inner peace and joy will be mission impossible.

I was making the same mistake for many years, this got me very frustrated and confused. I used to ask myself why others were getting ahead and becoming successful while I was doing almost everything right but still getting the same results. In my mind I thought reading and learning were enough actions required for me to achieve my goals. If you learn something and you don't apply or practice it, your chances of forgetting what you have just learnt are extremely high.

Information without activity and motion is seldom kept and maintained. Energy and action are related, the more energy, the more action and conversely, the more action, the more energy. We all want more out of life and to get more out of life, the only way is to apply massive action.

What happens if you do not do enough? Will you be able to live life on your own terms? My belief is that you live an extraordinary life, the moment you live life on your own terms and that also means you are fulfilled. Why not design your own path to light and perform actions that are aligned to your vision, acts that will lead you to a well-designed destination full of everlasting light, joy and inner-peace? *"Action without vision is only passing time, vision without action is merely day dreaming, but vision with action can change the world."* - by Nelson Mandela.

"Obedience to the laws of success leads to massively aligned actions which will guarantee massive success, joy and inner peace."

- Pheello Ntuka

Be transformed by choosing The Path to Light.

Some Key Points To Remember

An action is doing the work to achieve a specific goal.

Knowledge is the potential power, but applied knowledge is real power.

Too much information leads to confusion and distractions.

Actions speaks louder than words.

Obeyed laws lead to specific set of outcomes (Narrow path that leads to success)

Disobeying laws lead to undesired actions which will eventually steal your joy and inner peace.

Obedience to the laws guarantee success, joy and inner peace for the laws direct you to perform specific well-planned actions.

Develop the ability to act today, not tomorrow.

Life is 10 percent what happens and 90 percent what you do about it.

Action is the mother of success, joy and inner peace.

Apply the baby steps process and delay instant gratification, this will guarantee you success, joy and inner peace (Slowly but surely).

My Personal Notes

"

"Obedience to the laws of success leads to massively aligned actions which will guarantee massive success, joy and inner peace."

Pheello Ntuka

About the Author

Pheello Ntuka is a family man, a husband and a father of four daughters. He and his wife have been married for over 18 years and live in Johannesburg. He grew up in a small township called Sharpeville near Vereeniging. He studied Electrical Engineering and obtained a National Diploma at the Vaal Triangle Technikon, now known as Vaal University of Technology. He also acquired four certificates in life coaching. He is currently studying for a degree in Theology, this is due to his passion for learning and practicing the basic principles and the laws of the Almighty Creator. He believes in the word of God.

His purpose in life is to serve God's people by transforming their lives through personal development, self-education, the word of God and proven life principles. He has been working for Telkom SA for over 21 years and enjoys his role as a manager. He was promoted three times since joining the company in 1998. He started at the level of technical officer and was later promoted into access network operation specialist.

In 2016 he was promoted to become a manager to lead a team of twenty-three members. His role includes, but is not limited to staff management, financial management, administration, training and coaching, performance development and innovation. He is still enjoying his role as a manager, a motivational and an inspirational leader. He would like to be known for the principle of "Learn, Practice and Teach", something he strongly believes in and lives by.

Pheello is passionate about sharing his knowledge and life experiences, teaching and helping ordinary people to become extraordinary by achieving their major goals in life. He believes this is part of his purpose in this world.

www.ingramcontent.com/pod-product-compliance
Lightning Source LLC
Chambersburg PA
CBHW022038190326
41520CB00008B/632